INDIANA
HISTORICAL SOCIETY
PUBLICATIONS

VOLUME 26
NUMBER 2

The travelers: *back,* Estella and Guy Copeland; *front,* their sons Burl and William, and Guy's mother Nancy Wells Copeland

OVERLAND BY AUTO IN 1913

Diary of a Family Tour from California to Indiana

by
Estella M. Copeland

Indianapolis
Indiana Historical Society
1981

Introduction

The adventure of travel across the great plains is a story most people associate with the great migrations of the 1840s and 1850s, in which Easterners traveled to California and Oregon in wagon trains lured by the prospect of gold. But in fact the return trip from the West was equally as difficult for those whose hopes had not been fulfilled, and the great migrations back and forth across the plains have continued to the present day. The adventure recounted in the present diary of overland migration takes place not in a wagon train going west in the 1850s but in a lone automobile coming back east in 1913.

Automobiles were no longer exactly novelties in the United States by 1913, and they were much improved machines in comparison with the primitive horseless carriages of a decade before. Still, by today's standards, the 1910 Mitchell in which the Guy Copeland family traveled from Watsonville, California, to their farm in Marion County, Indiana, was both primitive and carriagelike. Nevertheless, the major impediment to automobile travel was not the ungainly machine but the surfaces upon which it was expected to travel. In 1913 roads in America were, by and large, either execrable or nonexistent; across the plains they were mostly nonexistent.

Despite these impediments automobiles had begun to travel from coast to coast in 1903. Three separate excursions undertook the journey that year; the fastest time was fifty-three days. J. M. Murdock, a wealthy lumberman from Johnstown, Pennsylvania, drove his wife, three children (aged 18, 14, and 10), and a mechanic from Los Angeles to New York in the spring of 1908, taking thirty-two days. The next year Alice Huyler Ramsey drove the other direction, New York to San Francisco, with three women passengers as a promotional stunt for Maxwell-Brisco Company, who provided her with one of their automobiles. She was only the tenth driver to make the trip. John G. Monihan, a Philadelphia automobile distributor, led eleven automobiles and a repair truck on an ocean-to-ocean tour in 1911, beginning at Atlantic City and ending in Los Angeles. The tourists included "eight millionaires" and a "countess."[1]

Generally speaking cross-country automobile touring was a sport either for the wealthy or for daredevil promoters in 1913; it was not yet normally in the domain of the middle income family man. Nevertheless Guy Copeland, an Indiana farmer returning home after a disillusioning year attempting to settle in California, packed up his mother, his wife, and their young family —two little boys, aged eleven and eight—into a 1910 Mitchell, purchased secondhand the previous fall, and set off across the plains in May, 1913. They were among the pioneers of family automobile camping across the western plains. They traveled simply as a family unit in the family car. Fortunately, Estella Copeland, Guy's wife, kept a fairly detailed log of their experiences, and they recorded highlights of the trip with snapshots.

---

[1] John B. Rae, *The Road and the Car in American Life* (Cambridge, Mass.: MIT Press, 1971), p. 34; J. M. Murdock, *A Family Tour from Ocean to Ocean* (Detroit: Packard Motor Car Co., 1908); L. Berson, "What a Thrill to Take the Wheel," in *Ms.*, III (1975), 17; R. S. Monihan, "Ocean to Ocean—by Automobile!," in *American Heritage*, XIII (April, 1962), 55.

The result is a rare historical record of early automobile travel by an adventurous, very capable family.

Guy Copeland (1872-1933) was not exactly a typical Indiana farmer. Descended from pioneers and toolmakers, Guy and his older brother Charles were talented mechanics, experimenting with applications of steam power to farm equipment around the turn of the century.[2] Both boys were obliged to drop out of school early (they were twelve and fifteen) in order to help their ailing father with the family farm. Guy Copeland thus had a fairly grueling youth, laboring like a man from his early teens.

Always fascinated by new machines Guy Copeland purchased a bicycle—a Dauntless Pneumatic—in 1893 for the quite substantial sum of fifty dollars and toured on it to visit relatives in Minonk, Illinois, more than two hundred miles from Greenwood.

After their father's death in 1893, Charles and Guy purchased farm machinery and experimented with commercial fertilizer to increase farm production. Their partnership ended with Charles's marriage in 1898 and his subsequent moves to Oklahoma and Texas. In 1899 Guy married Estella McNutt (1879-1938), a young woman from nearby Greenwood. They purchased Charles Copeland's share of the farm and set up housekeeping along with Guy's mother Nancy Wells Copeland (1846-1932) on the old homestead. This potentially awkward arrangement apparently developed instead into a long-lasting and basically happy lifestyle.

Guy Copeland continued on his own to experiment with new

---

[2] Charles Copeland actually patented a power steering device for steam engines (Patent No. 394,460) in December, 1888, when he was nineteen years old. William Copeland, Jr., "Guy Copeland—1872–1933," typescript [1979]. Information on Guy Copeland comes from this document except where otherwise noted. The diary, pictures, and miscellaneous material cited in this publication are in the possession of William Copeland, Jr., and will hereafter be cited as the Copeland Papers.

developments in farm technology, often plunging heavily in debt and always working with the intense industry he learned as a youngster. He purchased both a mechanical fencemaker, the Hoosier Boy Wire Fence Machine, and an incubator in 1901, and he also began to ship fertilizer into Greenwood for resale to neighboring farmers. Guy purchased an additional sixty-five acres in Johnson County and devised a Rube Goldberg-like system of pullies, shafts, and belts to perform a number of farm tasks utilizing gasoline engine power.

The Copeland family also expanded. Sons were born in 1902 (William) and 1905 (Burl). But the spirit of adventure in Guy Copeland was apparently in no way dampened by the burdens of supporting his family and running his expanding farm operations. Letters from his brother in Oklahoma reporting opportunities in the West fired Guy's lively imagination, and he was already investigating land opportunities in North Dakota by around 1906. Another relative, his mother's brother George Wells, was writing enthusiastically from his orchard in California where he had settled many years before. In 1910 Charles Copeland visited Uncle George and later reported to Guy all the wonders he had seen:[3]

> . . . Now if I should try to tell you all that we saw and heard and did it would be a long story and after all you would not know much about California until you have seen it for yourself. It is a country full of surprises.
>
> I saw many things that I did not expect and expected many things that I did not see. For instance I learned that squirrels make their den in the ground and rats build their nest in trees.[4] We saw pumpkins

[3] Charles Copeland to Guy Copeland, November 7, 1910. Copeland Papers.

[4] Charles Copeland describes a variety of California ground squirrel which inhabits pastures, fields, rocky ridges, and slopes with scattered trees and a type of woodrat, also known as "packrat," which sometimes nests in live oak trees on the West Coast. William Henry Burt, *A Field Guide to the Mammals* (Boston: Houghton Mifflin Company, 1976), pp. 97, 167.

that I doubt if two men could lift and alders one foot in diameter.

We saw a 1000 acre ranch that rents for $1000.00 a year and within two miles of it there are 10 acre tracts that will rent for as much.

Uncle George has tomato vines 6 to 8 feet high, having set stakes and tied them up, and they were loaded with tomatoes. He says there has not been a time that he could not go in his garden and get cabbage.

California is a large state and what can be said of one part of it does not apply to another part of it at all. As I said the country about San Jose and Santa Clara seems to be adapted to prunes and apricots. The Pajaro Valley is apples, apples, and more apples. Conditions seem to be just right here for their production. I know of no place else where the apple crop is considered a certainty. It is a fruit that does not do well in a warm climate, and in a cold climate it is apt to frost after the trees have blossomed, but in the valley they have the cool climate with no danger of a killing frost.

Pajaro Valley (pronounced Pä-hä-rō) contains about 40,000 acres and is surrounded by mountains from 1000 to 1500 feet high except a little gap that borders on the ocean. They are so completely shut in that no storm ever reaches them, and a person would naturally suppose that a place like that would get awful hot in summer, but not so. At night a fog comes in from the ocean and settles over the valley and the trees will be dripping next morning like it had rained.

By nine or ten o'clock the fog will clear away, but it will perhaps be a little hazy till noon. The heat of the sun is thus warded off and they tell me they can wear a coat comfortably every day in the year and take an overcoat if they expect to be out after the sun goes down.

Now some people might think it an undesirable place to live where they have those fogs, but I never heard any one say that they thought it unhealthy.

One thing I didn't like is the way the country is laid out. There isn't a road, row of trees, house or anything in the valley that is laid out square with the world.

They are so particular when they put out an orchard that they have a surveyor set the stakes where the trees are to be put, but pay no attention to the cardinal points.

They have good roads even though they are crooked. They are all either oiled, graveled or Macadamized. They roll them down with a big steam roller and have a wide oval grade.

Most of the work is done by foreigners, there being many Portuguese, Slavonians, Japanese, and Chinese. Most all the work is done by contract. They will prune the trees for so much per tree—usually 10¢ to 15¢ per tree. It is their business and they are experts at their trade. Much of the packing is done by the Japanese, they are naturally very quick motioned. Each apple is wrapped in paper and packed the same as oranges and shipped all over the world. The freight on fruit from Watsonville to New York is only $1.00 per 100 pound.

Of the apple crop there is nothing wasted. What is not fit to pack goes to the drying house and the parings and cores go into the vinegar vats.

One thing that impressed me very forcibly is the lasting quality of their building material. (It is redwood). While it is a soft wood, it resists decay in this climate almost beyond reason. Much of the fencing here until recent years was made by splitting redwood pickets about 2 inches square and driving them in the ground about 4 inches apart and nailing a 1 x 6 plank near the top. Many of these fences they told me were put up 30 to 40 years ago and still are in a good state of preservation and it looks like they would last for many years to come.

We all went to the beach one day clam fishing with Uncle George. We had a great time and got about two bushels of clams in less than an hours time after the tide went out.

It seems to me that a person can live easier and cheaper here than any place I have ever seen. Uncle George says their chickens will make their living—eggs were 48¢ per dozen when we were there. . . .

. . . Well California is not all roses, although it certainly looks that way at first sight. They have more fleas to the square inch than any place I ever saw. Uncle George says his place was alive with them when he went there, but thinks he will soon be shut of them.

Then they have a gopher which works in the ground like a mole and it will kill a field of alfalfa in two or three years if you don't watch and keep them killed out. They have the San Jose scale[5] and other

[5] Charles was probably unfamiliar with gophers since they live primarily in the western United States. Like moles, they live in underground burrows. Burt, *A Field Guide to the Mammals,* pp. 124–28. The San Jose

fungus diseases to fight in their orchards, and Grace says she could never learn to like the Chinamen. Coal is very high, about $15.00 per ton, but everybody burns wood which is $10.00 to $12.00 per cord of 4 foot lengths. Crude oil is 85¢ a barrel.

But to make up for these disadvantages they have strawberries nine months of the year, and I saw 100 acre patches of them. . . .

Though California's population had increased 60 percent between 1900 and 1910, there were still only a few million people living there when Guy Copeland began seriously to consider moving west. The Southern Pacific Railroad Company had been urging easterners to resettle in California since the 1870s. Guy Copeland, inspired perhaps by his brother's letter, acquired a Southern Pacific promotional booklet entitled *California for the Settler,* in which it was argued that farmers were needed in California: "California wants, as never before, the educated, up-to-date farmer, and to such our soil and climate offer phenomenal returns. . . . There are great opportunities here for men who can bring with them a few thousand dollars." The combination of his uncle, his brother, and the Southern Pacific proved to be a persuasive one: by March, 1912, Guy Copeland was ready to give California a try.[6]

The tie to the old homestead was a strong one, however, and he was careful not to burn his bridges behind him. Copeland rented the farmland to a cousin and auctioned off his livestock

---

scale is a circular, grayish scale about one sixteenth of an inch in diameter resulting from insect infestation. Fruit trees are typical victims. Ephraim Porter Felt and W. Howard Rankin, *Insects and Diseases of Ornamental Trees and Shrubs* (New York: The Macmillan Company, 1932), p. 142.

[6] Robert G. Cleland, *California in Our Time* (New York: Alfred A. Knopf, 1947), p. 105; Felix Riesenberg, Jr., *The Golden Road: The Story of California's Spanish Mission Trail* (New York: McGraw-Hill, 1962), pp. 174–75; quotation from A. J. Wells, *California for the Settler* (San Francisco: Passenger Department Southern Pacific, n.d. circa 1910), p. 3. The last publication is in the Copeland Papers.

Guy and Estella Copeland, 1912

William and Burl Copeland before the sale of the Copeland livestock in 1912

The Copelands took the train to Watsonville, California, March, 1912.

to pay his debts and raise a stake for a land payment in California. The receipts from the sale amounted to more than $2,300. He carefully retained his tools and large machinery, and he kept up his payment on the new sixty-five-acre addition to his farm. But the Copelands closed their house, went to Indianapolis, and boarded the train westward.

Their destination was Watsonville, California, the home of Copeland's Uncle George Wells. Watsonville, as Charles Copeland had reported, was the trading center for the apple-growing Pajaro Valley. In 1912 the town boasted five thousand inhabitants, a hundred apple-packing establishments, two vinegar factories, and a cold storage plant.[7] Guy quickly found work as a mechanic in an apple dehydrating plant, and by early May he

---

[7] *Souvenir California Apple Show October 7–12, 1912,* booklet. Copeland Papers.

Guy Copeland built this house at Watsonville in less than a month, completing it on June 1, 1912.

The Guy Copeland family with California relatives. Burl and William stand in front of their parents, Grandmother Nancy Wells Copeland is second from left, and Uncle George Wells is at the far right. The two other women have not been identified.

and Estella had acquired a city lot for a new home. The lumber cost less than $500, and the house was completed by June 1, 1912. A few months later the couple purchased a used automobile, a 1910 Mitchell touring car with a 35 horsepower engine, for $500.

Automobiles were not yet common in California. Only 36,000 cars were registered in the state in 1910, and the first roads constructed especially for automobile traffic were not built until 1912. But the automobile was already capturing the imagination of Californians, and farsighted legislators were preparing to spend vast sums to improve the state's roadways. It would probably be fair to say that cars were more popular in California in 1912 than they were in Indiana, especially among rural Hoosiers. However, the automobile was still seen essentially as the rich man's toy, even in California, and the Copelands' investment in the machine was an imaginative and unusual move for people in their circumstances.[8]

Their strategy was to tour California when Guy's work schedule permitted and look for a promising land deal at the same time. It is not clear how far afield these excursions took them, though it was probably not far. They certainly got to nearby Monterey, then posed in their bathing costumes by the seaside. But their searches did not uncover any promising opportunities for desirable land purchase. With the Indiana homestead never far from his mind, California land seemed expensive and less desirable to Guy. Meanwhile the Copelands chafed at "city" life and longed for a familiar lifestyle.

By January, 1913, Guy was already inquiring about routes back home. He wrote to Charles for information about the feasibility of taking the Mitchell overland, first to Olustee, Oklahoma, to visit Charles, and then home to Indiana.

---

[8] Cleland, *California in Our Time,* p. 106; Earl Pomeroy, *In Search of the Golden West: The Tourist in Western America* (New York: Alfred A. Knopf, 1957), p. 126.

Burl and William with Watsonville playmate in the center

Apple pickers, Watsonville

Estella, William, and Guy at the beach

The Copelands toured the redwood country in their new automobile.

Charles was quick to respond to his brother's inquiries:[9]

Mr. Dunlap of Lawton was down yesterday and he told me quite a bit about the roads between here and Calif.

In the first place he said don't start until the Spring rains are over or you will be sure to have trouble. Wait until the first of May at least. I inclose a map which he marked out showing both the central and Southern route. If you come the central which he says is much the best road and best scenery out take the *Trans continental road,* which leads from San Francisco to Eley, Salt Lake City, Cheyenne, Denver, Colorado Springs, Pueblo. He has not been over the road from Pueblo to Olustee but says he thinks you will find good roads to follow about the direction of the Fort Worth & Denver R.R.

In the Mountain and plains country between San Francisco & Salt Lake he says you will find numerous ranch houses where you can put up at night and will always find good accomodations, can get gasolene or any thing you need. The longest stretch between ranch houses now is 52 miles, that is just west of Salt Lake in the Alkali desert, he says don't tackle that unless it is dry. If it happens to be wet you will Bog up and cant go at all. If dry it is smooth and solid as pavement. He says always carry plenty of water and some lunch in case of imergency. Mr. Dunlap says if you will mention his name that most of those ranchers know him. He ran an Olds car, 60 horse engines and weighed 3800 #.

He says the Mitchel is a heavier car in proportion to the size of its engines, but will make it all right. He has been over this central route once in a wagon before autos had come into such general use.

He also marked out the Southern route as he had traveled it as far as Albuquerker, N. M. from there he went to Trinidad, Colorado but said he thought the road from Albuquerker to Tucumcary and Olustee would be all right, and Im sure it would for so many come through from N. M. in wagons.

You can get a road guide before you start that will tell you all about the roads. I think perhaps you can get a road from Salt Lake direct to Colorado Springs, instead of going around by Cheyenne.

---

[9] Charles Copeland to Guy Copeland, January 11, 1913. Copeland Papers.

I noticed there was a wagon road paraleling the RR nearly all the time, but there is much desert in western Colo. and Utah and the other way might be the best.

Guy and Estella Copeland spent the next few months making preparations for the trip home. They joined the American Automobile Association, formed in 1902, and acquired the *General Map of Transcontinental Routes with Principal Connections* which the AAA published in 1912. They had already apparently decided upon the southern route across the plains, since the map's marked trails showed the options of leaving either from Los Angeles or San Diego. Although AAA attempted to minimize the difficulties of the trek across the West, the organization still advised "that at least two cars should travel fairly well together, especially in the sparsely settled regions of the West. In case of accident to one, the other car could either render immediate aid or go for medical assistance, water, gasoline, oil or food." As for equipment needed for overland travel, AAA recommended the following:[10]

a shovel and axe, a hundred feet of ¾-inch rope, block and tackle, and a tarpaulin. The likelihood of some mud east of the Rocky Mountains, and the certainty of some sand stretches and arroyos beyond, may make this much equipment practically a necessity.

Of course, a few spare parts for the car are advisable, and each car should start out with new shoes all around, and a couple of spares —all of the same size if possible, with the addition of about six inner tubes. Tires, with the possible exception of odd sizes, may be procured in the larger cities along the standard routes. Tents and cooking utensils are largely optional, as the tarpaulin may be used for shelter, and canned goods for lunches. It is, however, particularly necessary to be provided with blankets, a couple of 5-gallon South

---

[10] American Automobile Association, *Transcontinental Main-Traveled Routes and Their Principal North and South Connections* (New York: AAA, 1912). Copeland Papers.

African water bags (which must be thoroughly soaked before using) and a collapsible canvas bucket.

For those expecting to camp out a considerable part of the way, especially in the Southwest, additional equipment will, of course, be called for. In such cases we suggest a light Tenalite auto tent, with ground cloth attached, and a collapsible aluminum pole, a camp lantern, an aluminum cooking outfit, two blankets per person and an air bed, with air pillows. Most of these supplies need not be carried until reaching the far West. It is advisable to be provided with oranges, lemons or canned pineapples, and a quantity of sweet milk chocolate in cakes.

The route the Copelands chose—the "Trail to Sunset"—was described by AAA as "the best route for the fall and early winter" though "too hot in midsummer." It ran across Arizona and New Mexico, joining the old Santa Fe Trail to Kansas City, Missouri. "This route," AAA continued, "offers magnificent mountain scenery, Indian pueblos and reservations, prehistoric ruins, Mexican habitations, giant desert cactus and tropical

The Mitchell, known as "Pussy," with Burl, William, their mother Estella behind them (third from the left), and Watsonville friends

Friends assembled to say good-bye to the Copelands in May, 1913.

vegetation in the irrigated regions." Confidently AAA announced that the "Trail to Sunset" was being "rapidly improved," while admitting that "there are yet several very rough stretches and a lack of hotel accommodations in some parts of New Mexico and Arizona, necessitating two or three nights camping out." The organization estimated that thirty to forty days would be needed for the trip.[11]

Perhaps it was the lure of southern California—the Copelands' desire to see all the sights while they were still in the West and their interest in visiting Guy's cousin in Glendale—that persuaded them to take the southern route despite AAA's warning that it would be "too hot in midsummer." In any event they packed up the Mitchell, said good-bye to their Watsonville friends and relatives, and headed south on May 15, 1913. The

[11] *Ibid.*

travelers were Guy and Estella, aged 41 and 34, Nancy Wells Copeland, aged about 67, and William and Burl, aged 11 and 8.

Their vehicle was a substantial automobile. The Mitchell was a large, heavy machine, not by any means an "economy car" of its day. It sold new in 1910 for $1500 f.o.b. San Francisco. The engine had four cylinders that generated 30 to 35 hp, which meant, as Charles Copeland noted, that it was somewhat underpowered for its size, but it was very solidly built and capable of withstanding considerable abuse. The vehicle also apparently possessed a sort of personality, since the family referred to it by a pet name: "Pussy."

The Copelands had assembled a fairly complete collection of local road information for the southern route. These materials were not road maps in the modern sense but rough sketches showing distances between towns and landmarks to confirm that the tracks an automobile was following were the correct ones. For the first leg of their trip the Copelands acquired the *Pacific Road Guide* published in 1912 by a San Francisco insurance agent with maps drawn by E. Rawlins. It covered roads from Seattle to Yuma. A hard-covered volume published by the Arizona Good Roads Association led them across Arizona. From eastern Arizona to Albuquerque and the Santa Fe Trail the Copelands had only a simple "log" published by the Butler Auto Company of Albuquerque, giving mileages between landmarks and terse instructions to bear left or right. These three guides are in the Copeland Papers. From Albuquerque to Newton, Kansas, approximately 780 miles, the Copelands apparently had a guidebook for the Santa Fe Trail, which was also marked in places by colored rings on telephone poles. This latter guidebook, mentioned in the diary, is not among the many papers the Copelands preserved. From Newton, Kansas, they turned south on the Chisholm Trail for their journey to Olustee, Oklahoma. They had no printed guides or logs for most of this section of the trip, and they simply asked directions from Olustee to Wichita. They had acquired maps from Indiahoma, Oklahoma, to El Reno, Oklahoma, and from El Reno, to Wichita. They found good roads and apparently adequate markers from Newton, Kansas, to Kansas City, and had a Goodrich Route Book from Kansas City to St. Louis. At St. Louis they acquired *A Guide and Directory for Automobile Tourists for 1913,* which consisted mostly of advertisements and included only three very generalized maps and a log of distances between towns. For Indiana they had excellent maps and route guides in the *Goodrich Route Book* for Ohio and Indiana.

Estella Copeland began her diary on May 15, as the family left Watsonville, and made entries daily until they arrived in Indiana on July 24. She kept her record in pencil in a simple unlined writing tablet. After she returned, Mrs. Copeland revised her diary, making a new manuscript in a stenographer's notebook. The text below is from the first diary, with additional information from the later diary inserted in brackets.

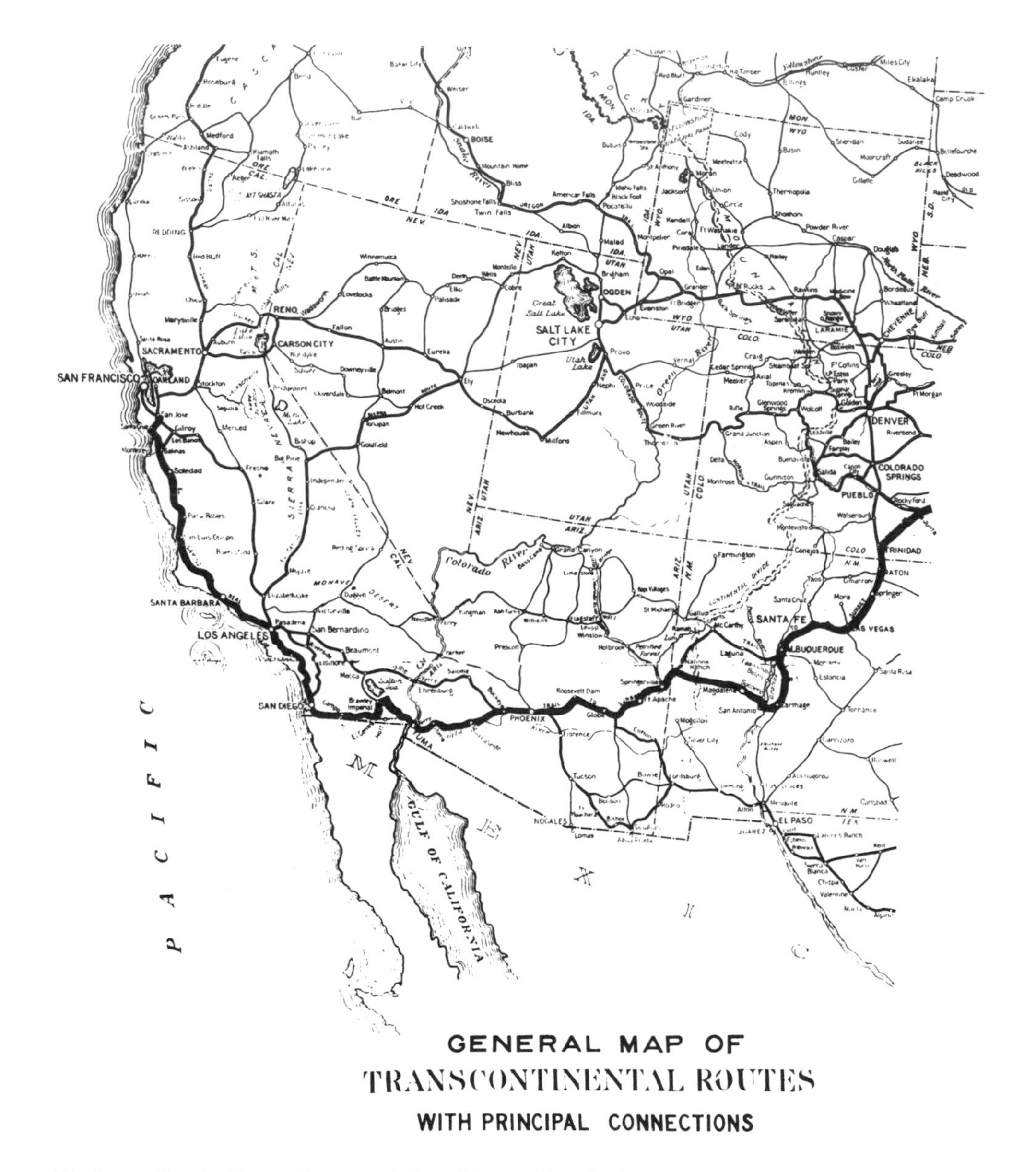

GENERAL MAP OF TRANSCONTINENTAL ROUTES WITH PRINCIPAL CONNECTIONS

The heavy line indicates the route followed by the Copelands: San Jose—Santa Cruz—Sabinas—Soledad—Paso Robles—San Luis Obispo—Santa Barbara—Los Angeles—San Diego—El Centro—Brawley—Yuma—Phoenix—Roosevelt Dam—Springerville—Magdalena—Socorro—Carthage—Albuquerque—Santa Fe—Las Vegas—Raton—Trini-

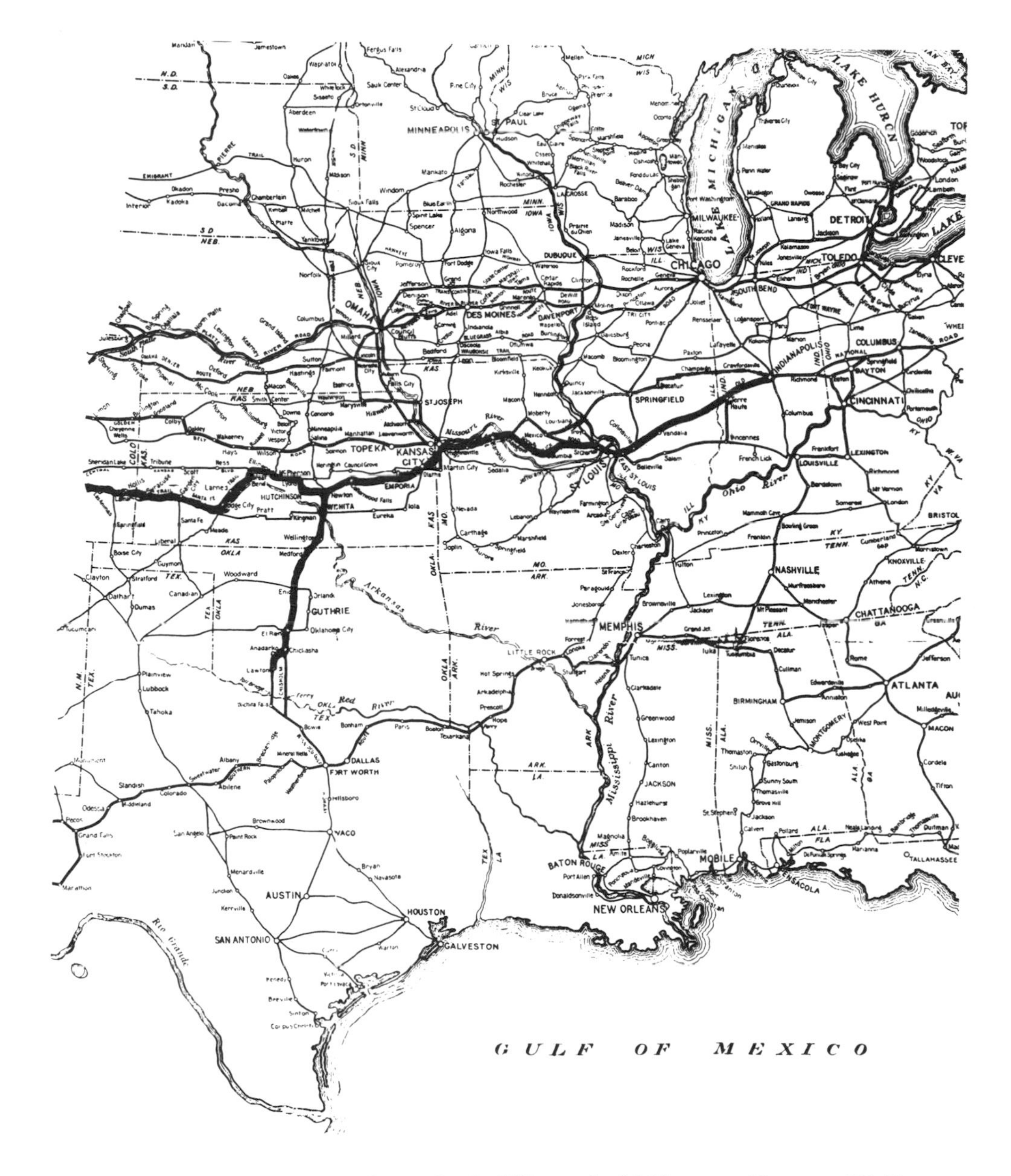

dad—Santa Fe Trail—Syracuse—Great Bend—Ellinwood—McPherson—Newton—Wichita—Medford, Okla.—Enid—El Reno—Lawton—back to Wichita—Kansas City—St. Charles—St. Louis—Vandalia—Terre Haute—Indianapolis

I

Watsonville, California, to Yuma, Arizona

May 15-26

12 days; 7 days traveling, averaging about 105 miles per day

The opening stage of the Copelands' journey was a relatively easy one. Dressed rather formally and in high spirits they stayed in hotels on their way to Glendale. But even in this early stage there were difficulties. The trip through the Santa Ynez Mountains had harrowing moments, and by the second day the steep grades had already proved too demanding for the 35hp Mitchell: except for the driver all the Copelands were obliged to walk while the machine labored up several hills. But the promise of better future roads was visible, since the Copelands found part of the new state highway completed near Delmar and a road crew working nearby.

In Glendale they visited Guy's cousin Emily Ribble Banta, a former Marion County schoolteacher, and her family and took a day to sightsee with their relatives in Los Angeles. They also found some of the Minonk, Illinois, relatives in Glendale and visited with them.

Guy Copeland also took advantage of the layover in Glendale to overhaul the Mitchell's engine. The Glendale Automobile and Machine Co. replaced two pistons and two pins, honed and packed the bearings, and replaced worn hoses at a total cost of $18.95. (Receipt, May 20, 1913. Copeland Papers).

They continued their relatively easy touring to San Diego, stopping at hotels and admiring the scenery. Their first night camping out came fifteen miles west of El Centro, California. Their tent was walled but had no floor. It only had room for four people, so Guy Copeland slept in the Mitchell that first night while his mother, wife, and sons slept in the tent.

The roads beyond Brawley were impassable because of quicksand, so the Copelands loaded their automobile onto a boxcar and took the train over the seventy-five-mile stretch to Yuma. It was at this point that Guy's mother Nancy Wells Copeland left the party, taking the train from Yuma to Olustee, Oklahoma, where she visited Charles Copeland and waited for the others to come overland. It is not clear whether Mrs. Copeland's departure at this point had been planned from the beginning with the realization that the journey beyond Yuma would be too rugged for the sixty-seven-year-old Mrs. Copeland, or whether it was simply the strains of the crowded car and a hint of hard traveling to come that convinced the group to change the plan at Yuma. In any event Grandmother Copeland left the party at Yuma and traveled in relative comfort the long journey to Olustee.

May 15. Left Uncle Geo. at 8.20 run 41 mi without a stop ate dinner [in the shade of a big oak] after crossing Salinas River first time at 11.45 distance of 50 mi. Then had about 8 miles of sand and it on the blow. All day we have watched the squirrels scamper in to the ground. got 1 gal. gasoline at Bradly, windy: forded the Salinas R. ate supper about 7 P.M. in edge of Paso Robles Spent night at the Ramona.

May 16. Left at 8.30 have had up grade and down grade all the way to San Luis Obispo went over the mountains. lots of sharp turns on our down side ate dinner a short distance out of S.L.O. close to a hot sulpher well 2200 ft deep just right for a hot drink It was capped to catch the gas for domestic purposes for a house close by At 3 P.M. were at Santa Maria

From Watsonville Cal to
Indianapolis, Indiana 1913
May 15 left Uncle Geo at 8.20 run
41 mi without a stop ate dinner after
crossing Salinas River first time
at 11.45 distance 50 mi. then had
All day we have watched the squirrels scamper
about 8 miles of sand and it on
the blow. got 1 gal gasoline at
Bradley windy: forded the Salinas R.
ate supper about 7 P.M. in edge of Paso Robles
Stayed night at the Ramona left
at 8.30 May 16 have had up grade
and down grade all way ~~all the way~~
to San Luis Obispo went over the
mountains lots of sharp turns
on our down side ate dinner a
short distance out of S.L.O. close to
a hot sulpher well 2200 ft deep just
right for a hot drink It was capped
to catch the gas for domestic purposes
for a house close by

First page of Estella Copeland's original diary

stopped about 5 minutes every thing O.K. roads now are sandy and Partly oiled real spoungy now at 4.45 roads are better; gravel, and we start on the climb of the Foxen Canyon got up very well till we come to the 20% pitch were on intermediate tried to change to low but Pussy didn't like that, we got out (all but Guy he tends the brake) find the drean-cock has jarred

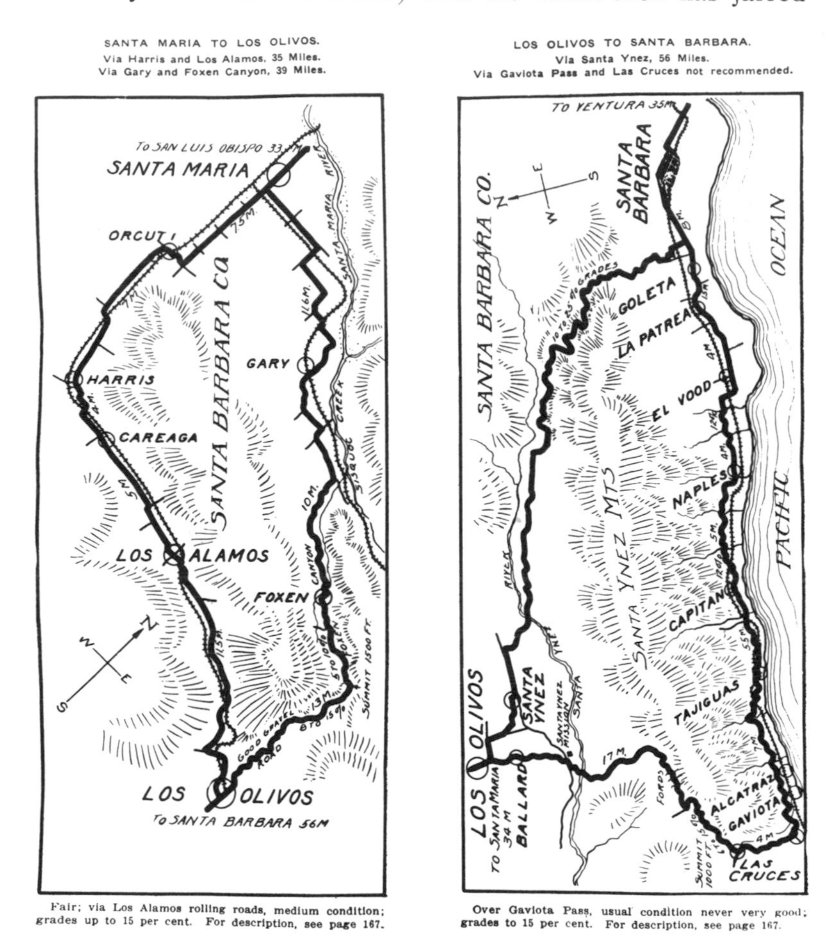

Two pages from *Pacific Road Guide*. Despite the *Guide*'s warning, the Copelands traveled through the Santa Ynez Mountains over the Gaviota Pass.

open have lost much water, had some in bucket Pussy takes holt on low but we limber up on a walk for a little way have got down quiet a ways find we are out of water; a family come along in Auto takes Guy in machine to get water its about 6 P.M. and here he is has been gone about ½ hr. its only about 1¼ mile to Los Olivos a "one horse" town we spent the night here.

May 17. Left May 17 about 7.45 came over the Gaviota Pass the Pacheco Pass is tame to what much of the road has been since Paso Robles The road this A.M. has been curves, dangerous too; are stopped for dinner 12.30 not far from Santa Barbara have come only 47½ miles The trunk-rack has a broken iron is getting doctored by wood and wire the road now is like a paved street. After passing through Santa Barbara instead of keeping on the sea-beach road we turned left towards the mountains, well say we sure did get experience going through the Casitas Pass there is just a very small valley between the East and West Casitas curves very short, numerous and close together came near bumping unto another machine, he was comming up faster than we were going down got to Ventura about 7 P.M. spent the night at the Green Tavern was tired only traveled about 75 miles.

[*May 18*]. Left at 6.45 over fine roads a fine boulevard most of the way to Glendale went by the way of Lankershim on Centeral Ave. to Burbank on this ave we found deep sand got to Glendale about 2 P.M.

Monday May 19. Emmaline Monroe-Grover and little daughter Emmaline Jane spent the day with us at Emma Banta's in the evening Mr. & Mrs. Leonard and Ada Monroe called.

Tue. May 20. Maria & Emma, Wm., Guy & I went to Los Angeles saw Mrs. Butterfield & Maud, also Homer Hittle when we got back to Glendale there was Clara Monroe-Darlington to see us; in the evening we went over to Mr. Lenard's (they were Minonk, Ill. people).

Wed. May 21. Up Early this A.M. gathering up our belong-

Estella and the boys amidst the rocks

ings ready for to start Eastward; Edna Lenard called a few minutes Maria baked a cake for us, it was fine 8.30 A.M. we are on the road again go through Los Angeles by the way of 7th St. pass through fine orange country [nearly every grove the ground is covered with frost bitten oranges but the trees through here generally were saved by smudg pots] the roads are O.K. some grades once in a while but nothing bad, ate dinner at edge of Santa Ana that is beautiful country; two back tires were a little flat when got into Oceanside at about 6 P.M. Guy has put in new inner tubes and all are ready for a good night's rest at the Booth Hotel.

Thursday May 22. Well we didn't rest so good, too many misquotes! Got started about 8 A.M. for San Diego when several miles out stopped on the rocky beach and made a fire for hot water for breakfast. Found part of the State Highway completed its fine but at Delmar we found the construction gang had rather bad sand getting round them then we came to a very steep sandy grade Pussy balked a little, all got out but Guy; Ma & Boys walked on I staid to help with car, it soon went off O.K. we soon took on all passengers and clumb to the top, we had boiling water when we got there [filled up the radiator with water from the construction gang's tank,] soon we came to La Jolla here the flowers have the most beautiful coloring have saw any where in Cal. this is a Sea resort. reached S. Diego at noon am disappointed in this country expected to find orange groves haven't found any yet. We walked a way out on the pier saw a large U.S. Army repair ship which had been in this harbor for 4 yrs. also saw some torpedo boats and the U.S.A. vessel Denver. There was a steam boat from Old Mexico taking on freight. To night we have nice rooms for 75 cts a room that's the most reasonable we have found.

May 23. Well we got a good start from San D[iego] this morning for El Centro 125 miles eastward good solid road-bed for 83 miles but round and round on a mountain shelf most of the time but the last stretch that is after you pass Campo is a wonderful piece of road engineering These mountains are just heaps of rock [and a shelf has to be blasted out to make the road]; the road way, with many a quick turn, follows the canyon known as the Devil's Canyon then we come right out in deep sand Pussy pulled right through there were signs all along the way telling how far to water, it finally began to get dusk and still on the desert, about 1 mile from water we met a

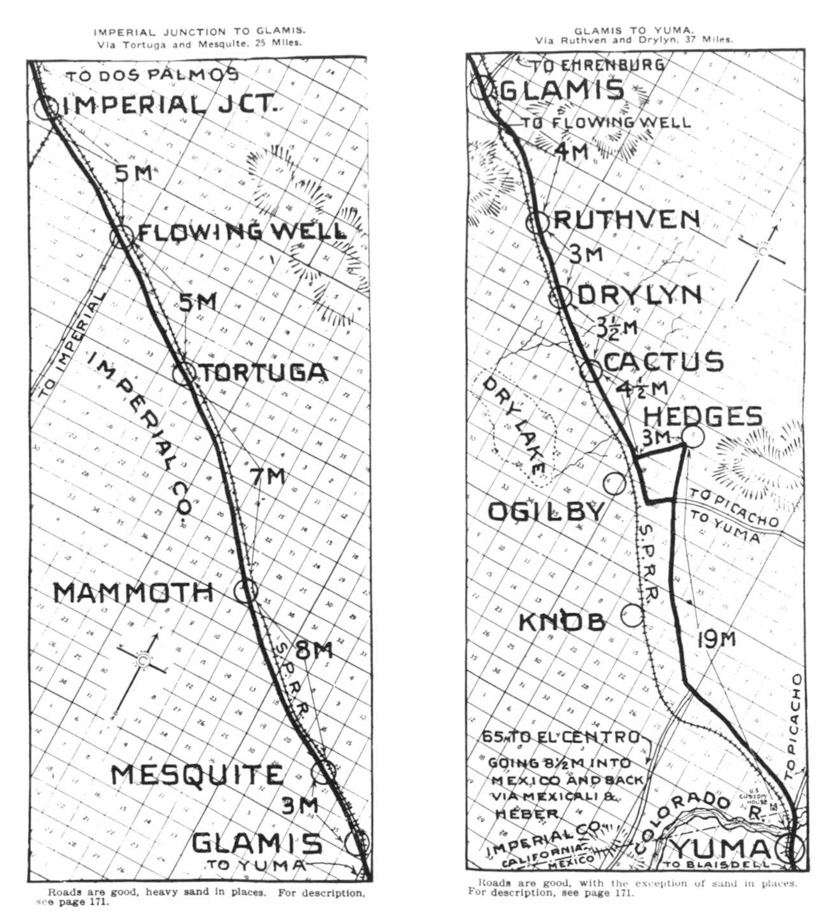

Two pages from *Pacific Road Guide*. The Copelands and the Mitchell traveled this section of the trip by train.

big motor truck with about 7 men all seemed to be drinking we didn't talk long to them, we before long came to a little new town [called Dixie Land] but as El Centro was only 15 miles, and that didn't seem like a very good place to stop we went on for about a mile only, when an oilman stopped us said we couldn't get by his wagon stuck in the road, well we went back to that undesirable place pitched our tent by the side of the street [by the side of a feed-lot (place run like a livery stable)] in soft sand all crawled in the tent but Guy he thought it better to sleep in the car. [tell you it was a "tough" place].

May 24. [Its an early start for El Centro only 15 miles away and part of the road is good, some is through deep washes; we have been warned not to undertake to cross the Mammoth Wash as three Autos are now stuck in the sinking sand, but we learn at El Centro that the roads are good 17 miles farther on to Brawley] Well here we are about a mile from Brawley, in camp expect to stay here till Monday morning then we ship the car and ourselves to Yuma, [lost no time pitching the tent so we could shed some clothes only yesterday, wore our overcoats Today its 100 in the shade.] have just opened the box Ella gave us it was so nice of her to think of us that way we sure do appreciate it.

May 25. Laid around all day trying to keep cool T'was 98 deg. in the shade, we are 119 ft below sea level, the water is sure "bum," right out of the irrigating ditch, [all comes from the Colorado River which is very muddy; The water is dipped up into a large vessel let settle] makes one have a weak feeling about the stomach. This is a very fertile valley much alphalfa, horses, cattle and hogs [train load after train load of cattle was shipped here this spring from the drought stricken pasture lands of Calif.] also field after field of cantalopes; see plenty of Japs, several Hindos.

May 26. Up early this morn are here at the station now 9.45 A.M. Think the auto is about loaded Just before leaving this evening found out that in this locality, in trying to make wells

Waiting in Yuma for the train to leave

they get salt water. 6 P.M. Still here at this low down town, have been to a resturant for supper the place is run by Japs but their strawberry-shortcake and coffee tasted very well just the same [its been so very hot today 110 in shade] I was uncermoniously wakened from a nap this afternoon, about 3 oclock, by an earthquake. Our train for Yuma leaves at 7.40 this evening.

II

Yuma, Arizona, to Springerville, Arizona

May 27–June 13

12 days, 470 miles, averaging less than 40 miles per day

The earthquake Estella Copeland reported in Brawley on May 26 was the first in a long series of disturbing experiences the Copelands were to undergo in the next few stages of their journey. Between Yuma, Arizona, and the New Mexico-Colorado border, the Copelands were traveling through extremely rugged terrain on "roads" that were in fact usually only rough trails.

Immediately beyond Yuma they encountered a countryside that was unfamiliar and often alarming. Estella Copeland comments in fearful tones on the presence of Indians and Mexicans. The family quickly find themselves stuck in sinking sand and begin a soon-to-be familiar and wearing pattern of unpacking and pushing the Mitchell through heavy sand and up steeply graded hills. After Yuma the Mitchell loses its nickname "Pussy" and becomes simply "the auto." Water is scarce; the sand blows so fiercely they cannot see to drive; and gas costs 50 cents a gallon. Eleven-year-old William Copeland became ill, probably from heat and exhaustion, on May 31. He was unable to keep food in his stomach for three days and was not recovered until June 5.

Fortunately at Globe, Arizona, on June 1 the Copelands encountered another family traveling along their road, and for the next three and a half weeks the two parties joined forces in their struggle through the desert and mountains of Arizona and New Mexico. The newcomers were "2 men & 2 women and a fox terrier." The older couple were Mr. and Mrs. DeLamater of Bethel, Connecticut, experienced automobile tourists. Mr. DeLamater was a wholesale druggist and perfumer, "Manufacturer of the Famous 'Diana' Greaseless Cream." His son William, a physician, and the son's fiancee, a Miss Madeline Klinge from New York, comprised the younger couple. The dog was named Teddy.

The availability of the assistance of two grown men, one of them a doctor, lifted the Copelands' spirits and probably contributed materially to William's chances for surviving the trip. The two parties encountered few other automobiles across Arizona. In Springerville merchant Julius Becker, whose store was a way station for tourists on the Ocean-to-Ocean Highway, informed Guy Copeland that only nineteen automobiles before them had registered as crossing the White Mountains in 1913.[1]

May 27. We got to Yuma last night about 11 o'clock. Went to the Arizona Hotel Ma left about 8 A.M. for Chas. [Olustee, Oklahoma] lots of Indians in this place rather a tough looking people, in general, the man at the garage told us how to go the best road, it sure was bad as soon as you are out of the dirty town of Yuma it is desert, My! but it is warm, Think we were about ten miles out struck a rut, heard a noise and our trunk sat in about 6 inches of dust, the straps holding it had got so hot they had expanded and slipped off, well! we soon got straightened up and on our way at about 20 miles we came to Dome P.O. The railroad is here that and a few Indians is all, the Post M. and sta[t]ionmaster of course are white, out of Dome we soon come to the Gila River [dry river bed] here we got stuck in the sinking-sand had to cut brush, for to make a road-way then jack up

---

[1] Tucson *Arizona Daily Star*, May 7, 1950. Clipping in Copeland Papers.

The Copelands' guide through Arizona

Instructions for the use of Road Maps and Key to Symbols

These maps are not drawn to a scale though the relative locations of towns and scenes are regarded. They are logs of the roads made while traveling in an automobile and devised to give every necessary detail to keep a traveler on the roads he intends following. The worst features of all roads are recorded so that he may know just what conditions to prepare for.

Refer to the Index map often, especially at important road forks and at the end of a route shown on a page.

Photographs of land marks and the scenes where there is the greatest likelihood of taking the wrong road are on all map pages and will be easily recognized when the place is reached. In many pictures the Road Mapping Car is visible and unless otherwise indicated, it stands on the main road the map refers to.

Distances are measured from Post Office to Post Office in nearly every instance.

Where a double road is shown for a short distance, the heavier line will lead over the better and easier grades.

Special city maps of many cities and towns will be found of great value in entering or leaving by the best roads. The numbers on these maps show the location of the Hotel, Garage, Bank or Business House which has a corresponding number on it's photograph.

SYMBOLS

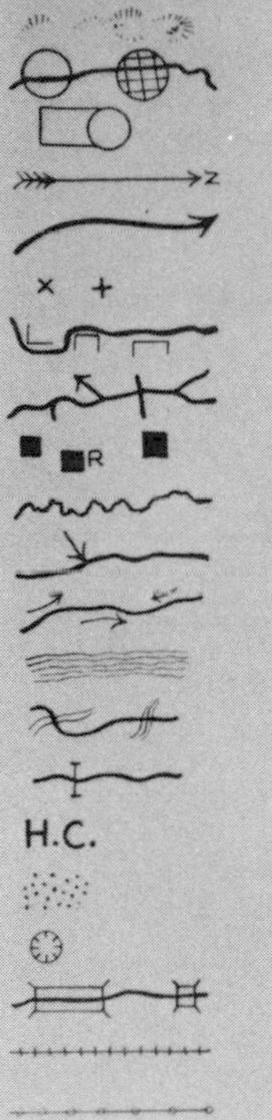

Mountains or Hills.

Cities and towns the road passes through.

When traveling northerly or westerly, mileage from starting point is in the square; southerly or easterly, in the circle.

Approximate north.

Arrows lead from the pictures to the place on the road where the fork, landmark or scene is located.

Crosses: Location of sign post or board.

Fine angle lines: Fences at side of road.

Short diverging lines: Road forks or crossings.

Dark squares: Buildings. When with an "R," ranchhouse, with P. O.," postoffiice.

Wavy line: Crooked road.

Arrow at right angle with road line gives location of apex of divide or summit.

Small arrows indicate grades and point up hill. Percentages are given at particulary steep places.

River. Each is marked by a bridge or ford.

Washes and gutters crossing road.

Location of gate passed through.

High Centers.

Dots: Sand. H. S. is added where sand is heavy.

Corral near road.

Bridges.

Railroad track. Steam or electric.

Telegraph, telephone or power line.

[p. 7 from guide]

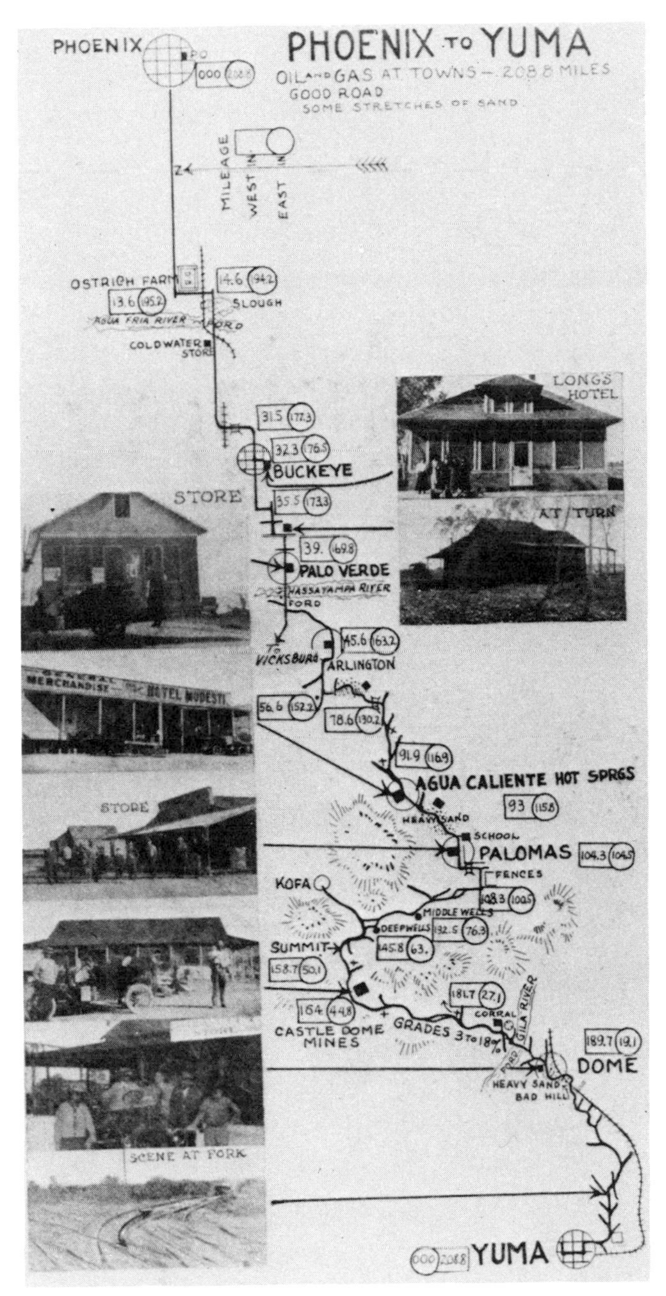

[p. 50 from guide]

the wheels, we worried along that way going a little piece at a time, we heard another machien stuck back of us after while here they came two Indians hitched their ponies on by their larettes wound around their saddle horns (it was a Ford Auto with two men) we were almost out of the river so we gave the same Indians $.50 to get us out; The Ford Auto is going to Phoenix, too, so we will have company if they don't want to run too fast; we soon strike lava beds better road, but hard on tires, not bad so we run awhile by lamp-light the other auto is ahead don't see it so stop for night way out here to our selves, don't see what even a grass hopper could live on have come about 36 miles this afternoon.

May 28. Up early going to go a while before breakfast think will come to fresh water Pass our Ford Auto they are eating breakfast only about ¾ of a mile from us; we run about 10 miles when we come to Castle Dome Lead Mine, the well is over 300 ft deep, good water here we eat breakfast. there are only about half dozen buildings but they all seem to be occupied by American people [nice looking people] saw 3 different women, one we talked to was a very inteligant woman they gave us a sample of ore and what it is taken from; now we must fill up well with water for will not find any more for 65 miles, it only took about 4 gal for drinking an[d] engine, but the roads are awful, lava beds then desert sand [Find by the road side what looks like a grave with the word HERBERT made with rocks about the size of hen eggs and miles farther another place that is much the same but marked "Mama"] we finally came to the Palomas store about 2 P.M. here we Paid 40 cts per gal. for gasoline we had lost some time helping the Ford Auto patch a blowout the country round Palomas was once, a few years ago, under cultivation but their dam broke and things were deserted the ground is rich, so Uncle Sam has a camp here now planning an irrigating system. Here too we find a fellow, who looks to be about 35, repairing his motor cycle-tire he has come from San Diego is going to New York He motored across the Mammoth Wash or Big Desert

Ostrich ranch near Phoenix

said they told him he could not but he did. My! but the wind is blowing, fine sand is deep, we in crossing a little dry creek got in sand, Ford Auto men come back to us and we get brush under the back wheels Guy runs the auto the rest push and out it goes. A desert dust storm is not pleasant. Not any fun to have to wait for a thin place in the dust so you can see how to drive The Ford Auto man is having a time with his tire it is about done for, its our time to help him, he is from Santa Ana, Cal. About 3 P.M. we pull up in front of the Aqua Calentine [ed. Caliente] Hot Springs the water is hot soda water they cool it the Ancient Egyptian way, an earthen jar in this shape[2] wrappen in grain sacks and hung in the air, good and cool, too, we are yet 86 miles from Phoenix, nothing here but the Springs. On we go over desert sand then lava beds are getting a little higher up on what is called this Mesha camp up here after dark have tried to make Arlington the next water but fail our Ford auto goes on they say they have 10 cars of mules waiting them.

---

[2] Here Estella Copeland draws a line sketch of the jar.

May 29. Up at daylight run about 15 miles then we come to our first farming land [since left Imperial Valley Calif.] its only 48 miles from here to Phoenix here an irrigating ditch has broke and the road is muddy get part the way through its awful slippery so have to put on the chains to finish a man tell us we will find good water at a school house about a mile down the road here we eat breakfast. On to Phoenix can't tell what time it is for Guy got his watch hands turned last night see the rail road at 31 miles from Phoenix first time since 20 miles out of Yuma. Several Ostrich ranches where there are large herds of the ugly birds. got into Phoenix about 12.30 Had used something near 16 gal of gasoline in the 208 miles run awful dirty get a room take [buy] a bath eat a lunch then lay down the rest of the afternoon wrote some cards and when we went to a resturant for supper find have dated them all wrong for had lost just one day some where.

May 30. [Went out on the street this A.M. find flags at half mast wonder the cause, find out its Memorial Day, we are all twisted about days of week] Laid in supplies this A.M. it is 1 o'clock now will start soon. They tell us we have come over our worst road. Got started at 3 P.M. good roads Its the Santa Fe trail, for a few miles out fine farming country irrigated by the great Roosevelt Dam raise much alfalfa fine cattle and hogs, part of their cotton looked about 10 inches high, part of their wheat is cut its fine, too. We had some desert before we began to climb the mountains stopped for the night at 6:30 P.M. way up in the mountains about 40 miles from the Dam had run 39 miles.

May 31. Up and started about 6 A.M. up grade around curves part the time we are running on top of the big hills, some cooler up there, real warm down in the canyons, we met some people moving from Roswell, N.M. to Cal. in wagons looked to me like a great big job. The senery is fine, we took a picture but it will not begin to tell the beauty [but O' such a dangerous road just one little some thing wrong and we would

"We have desert, with much rock and plenty of heat." June 2, 1913

A pack train to mines near Globe, Arizona

land hundreds of feet down among the rock.] come to Roosevelt Dam about noon walk over and take a look it is a most wonderful piece of man's hand-work, God gave them the material right there [if he hadn't it never would have been built, nothing could have been brought over such road as it is to the nearest rail road, Phoenix, 79 miles] the stone side of the mountain makes part of the dam, their stone slabs were cut from the mountain's side, even have their own cement factory their overflow comes through two large holes in the mountain side and it makes a beautiful waterfall, which would judge to be 100 [ed. feet?], took 5 yrs to build this great water harness (was begun in 1906 dedicated in 1911 by Theo Roosevelt) we got to Globe late afternoon Wm. is real sick; camp out [under a tree] near the City water works. This is a copper mining city of about 10 000 population notice the people most all look so small.

June 1. Wm. still vomiting, we feel blue; about noon an auto drives up with 2 men & 2 women and a fox terrier [Mr. De-Lamater and wife & son Dr. Wm. and Miss Madeline Klinge and dog Teddy] a Los Angeles banner, Guy goes over to talk to them finds out they are bound for New York that they cross the U.S. every year and know the road we feel better. After they get their camp established the young man comes over calling he is a doctor thinks Wm. will get all right after a dose of castor oil, we have planned to stay together. The older man is Vice-President of the American Auto Association, name is DelMonte [DeLamater].

June 2. Wm. still feeling badly, the Dr. says too much sun. we leave Globe about 9:30 A.M. are going by Springerville. Its 20 miles to Rice roads are very good Mr. DelMounter's loose their large water bag we find it, so they are O.K. Rice is an Indian villiage The government has an Indian school here.[3] We have desert, with much rock and plenty of heat Begin our

---

[3] This school in Rice was operated for the Apaches on the San Carlos Indian Reservation. James E. Officer, *Indians in School: A Study of the Development of Educational Facilities for Arizona Indians* (Tucson, Arizona: The University of Arizona, 1956), p. 13. Rice was later renamed and became the new location of the town of San Carlos when the original settlement was threatened by flooding from San Carlos Reservoir. *Arizona: A State Guide*, compiled by Workers of the Writers' Program of the Work Projects Administration in the State of Arizona (New York: Hastings House, 1940), p. 447.

climb at Rice at 36 miles we reach Cassador Springs here we cool our engines, fill up with water. The Boys and I go wading, and Mr. DelMonte give Teddy dog a bath at 3:30 P.M. we start on, [our guide book tells us have] a very steep 4 miles climb before us till we reach a camping spot, the road is very narrow but not much traveled: [we have to walk and push part time] It took 2 hrs to get to the top; we traveled 40 mi used 49 gal of gasoline The Dr. killed Wm. a wild pigeon which we broiled for his supper, but he didn't keep it down long. Its a beautiful camping spot up here in the timber a grand view of the desert we came over.

June 3. We tried to start at 6 this morning but Mr. Delmounter's engine balked, but at 8 we were off My! but its grand to be traveling in among the trees and smell the pine about 9.30 we reach the resedence of the Supt of the San Carlos Indian reservation we have to pay $1 to go through the gate [the Supt. said the money was to make the road, but surely not much is used on it for its only a trail] we get a quart of milk for 15 cts and a dozen of eggs for 45 cts but we need them for Wm. These rocky gulches are simply awful, can hardly get through Mr. Delmounter's engine still acts rather balky. we met a man, his wife, daughter and parrot in a Ford Auto enroute from Franklin, Neb. to Los Angeles Then on we go, have only went about 10 miles and its 11.30 but its a fine place to eat dinner Wm. kept his egg nog down Mr. Delmounter's have a blow out at 3.30 P.M. we get to Black River, Ariz. There was a store here but not any one about but the Kitty and Collie pup everything has the appearance of a hurried exit even cooked meat in the frying pan. [this is the first house have seen in miles and miles] The Dr. is not very well we have a good camping spot, so stay Wm. has got turned against his milk, can't find any wild birds for to make him broth so as there are 4 young chicks of about 1½ lb the Dr. says better kill one so we do, make a good broth he took some then slept all night At dark an Indian came he staid all night. Mrs. D. is cooking beans they keep

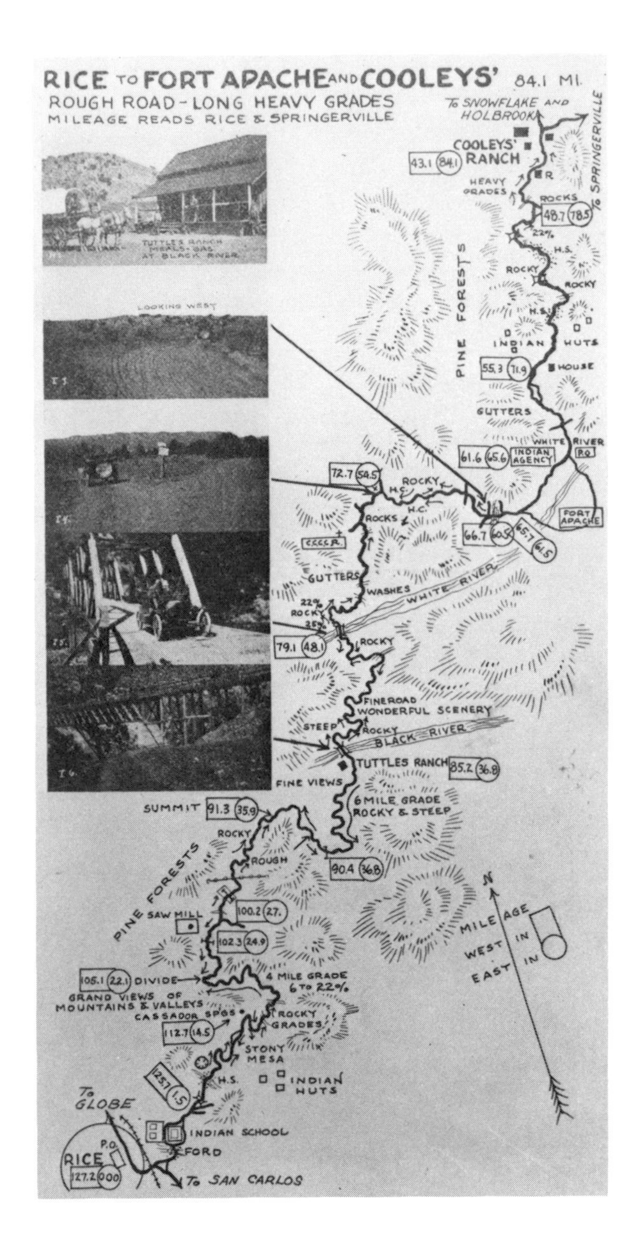
RICE TO FORT APACHE AND COOLEYS' 84.1 MI.
ROUGH ROAD - LONG HEAVY GRADES
MILEAGE READS RICE & SPRINGERVILLE
TUTTLES RANCH MEALS-GAS AT BLACK RIVER
LOOKING WEST
To SNOWFLAKE AND HOLBROOK
To SPRINGERVILLE
COOLEYS' RANCH
43.1 84.1
HEAVY GRADES
ROCKS
48.7 78.5
22%
H.S.
ROCKY
ROCKY
PINE FORESTS
INDIAN HUTS
55.3 71.9
HOUSE
GUTTERS
WHITE RIVER P.O.
61.6 65.6
INDIAN AGENCY
72.7 54.5
H.C.
ROCKY
H.C.
ROCKS
66.7 60.5
65.7 61.5
FORT APACHE
GUTTERS
WASHES
WHITE RIVER
22%
ROCKY
25%
79.1 48.1
ROCKY
FINE ROAD WONDERFUL SCENERY
STEEP
ROCKY
BLACK RIVER
TUTTLES RANCH
85.2 36.8
FINE VIEWS
SUMMIT
91.3 35.9
6 MILE GRADE ROCKY & STEEP
ROCKY
ROUGH
90.4 36.8
PINE FORESTS
SAW MILL
100.2 27.
102.3 24.9
N
MILEAGE
WEST IN
EAST IN
105.1 22.1 DIVIDE
4 MILE GRADE 6 TO 22%
GRAND VIEWS OF MOUNTAINS & VALLEYS
CASSADOR SPGS
112.7 14.5
ROCKY GRADES
STONY MESA
125.7 1.5
H.S.
INDIAN HUTS
To GLOBE
INDIAN SCHOOL
P.O.
RICE
127.2 0.00
FORD
To SAN CARLOS

swelling and swelling her kettle won't hold them all so some has to be thrown away. We don't go to bed very early would rather not have had company but he seems tame.

June 4. [Wm. much better this A.M.] Got up about 5; Mrs. D. gave the Indian his breakfast Then he was off. We got started 6.30 [have to climb a mountain first thing] Did not get far till Mr. D.'s had a blow out finally got on again. Another blow out for Mr. D.'s about 10 A.M. here we change 3 tires while are at it a cowboy comes up has his pack mule, the horse he is riding jumps down about a 6 foot embankment. its right straight down, all the damage done was hurting the boy's sore thumb a horse had kicked him about 3 weeks before never healed, the Dr. examines it finds he has a nice case of blood-poisening, he dressed it with peroxide, hope it gets well; this is a wild, wild country many, many miles from a Dr. but its some warm 90 deg. The Dr. has such a lame back to day he is about all in. we get started again go about 2 miles they have another leaky tire, we eat lunch here and get along again its up grade all the time, and such a road but once in a while we see a sign which reads Westgard's Trail to the Sunset but we do enjoy being among the trees and seeing the flowers by the way side (can't say road for its a trail) about mid afternoon we come in sight of Fort Apache but the road past there is not good so we don't go past saw some of the soldiers boys on horseback This is an Indian reserve for the Apache Indians, said to be the wildest and most obstinate tribe of all That why the soldiers here to keep them off the war path, only about 1½ miles farther is White River a little villiage here we get a few needed supplies, sugar is 2 lb for .25 we get Wm. some rice .10 cts per lb. he is not well yet but a little better, about half dozen Indians [in bright colors] gather about the machines. Soon we go onward but not very swift for are still going upward and our engines get hot very quickly, about 4 P.M. Mr. D. thinks we better stop for the night but there is quite a hill before getting down to the river should judge a mile walk and

RIGHT OF WAY PERMIT

SAN CARLOS INDIAN AGENCY

San Carlos, Arizona, [illegible] 3 191[illegible]

Mr. [illegible] of [illegible] Arizona, is hereby permitted

to drive 1 automobile, — head of cattle, — head of horses, — head of mules,

— head of burros, across the San Carlos Indian Reservation, in accordance with the regulations

printed on the back hereof.

Fees Paid, $ 1.[illegible]

[illegible signature]

Superintendent.

as we have to have much water to night for Mr. D.'s wheel-rims have got so loose too much of a drying air, ours are in fairly good shape but want to water them any way. Move on for about 4 mi here Mr. D. has another blow out, we see Indians and their huts real often now. three men in a Ford Auto come along the driver warns us of bad sand but says follow his tracks and we will get through, we do. he also tells of a very steep climb before the sand its look about like This[4] we simply had to push both Autos up, plenty of rock in the trail too after we get through the sand we come to a brook with good water its late here we camp very tired, have not come many miles to day but we were fighting upward all the while.

June 5. Cool this A.M. hang the thermometer out its just 37 deg. Wm. is better, but the Dr. don't walk straight by quiet a bit. The men go all over the Autos so its 9 A.M. before we get on our way. don't go very far till here is another straight up hill if any thing worse than the evening before we unload our heaviest luggage every-body pushes all their might little by little both cars are at the top, you see we are not far from 9000 ft of an elevation air is very light about at the top of the hill is a trail to the Sunset sign, Ocean to Ocean Highway we all decide its a very poor one and not any fun going over it either. We get along nicely, have another hill but not so bad as the other two, we use the pushies behind though get to Cooley's Ranch at 11.45 he is a white man [and very sick] who married an Indian [they have two grown children]. At this place we meet 2 men from Kansas City enroute to Los Angeles give them a few instruction for which they are very thankful and they go on Their car has a 60 horse engine. After leaving here we get on the wrong trail get to Pine Top store here we get some ginger snaps 20 cts per lb but they are good very grumpy old store keeper though. A tire has to be repaired for Mr. D. so we

---

[4] Here Estella Copeland draws two parallel lines slanting sharply upward.

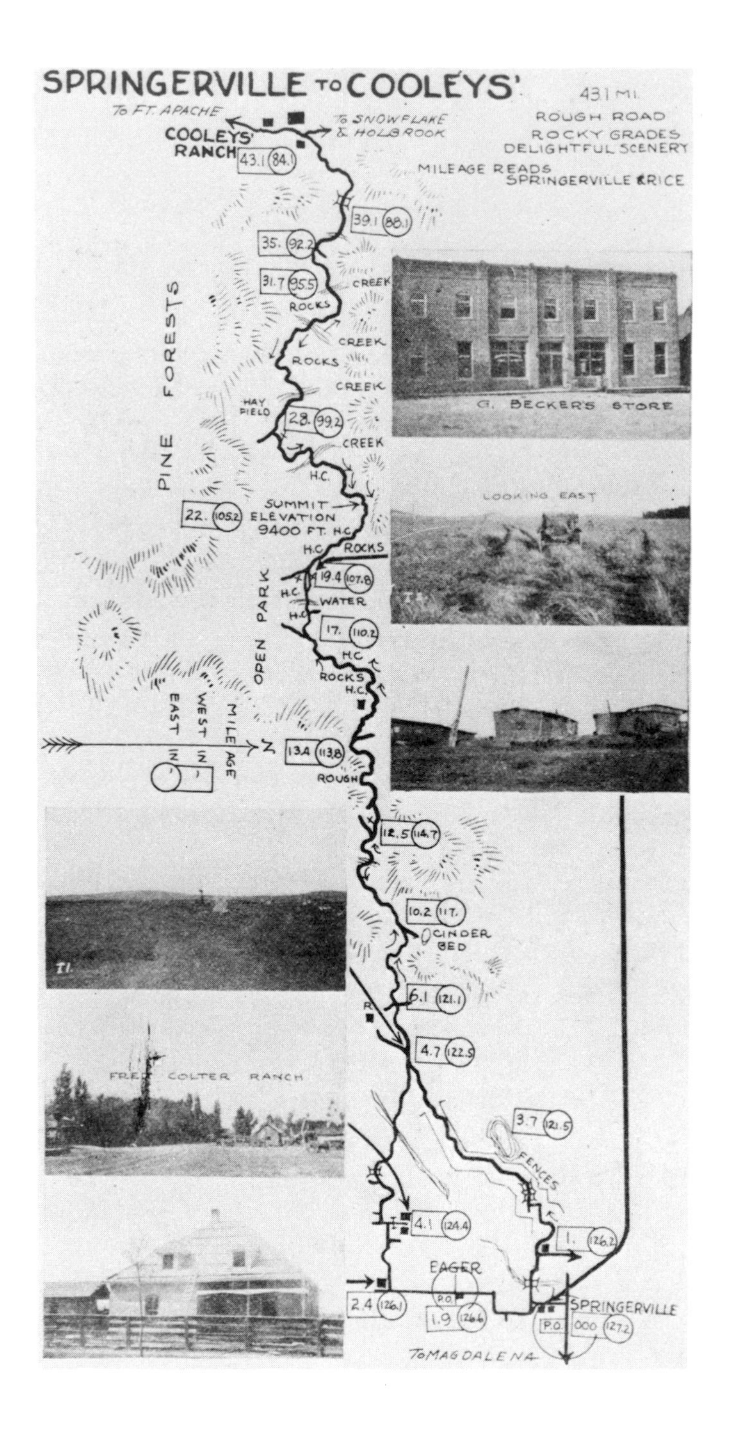
SPRINGERVILLE TO COOLEYS'
43.1 MI.
ROUGH ROAD
ROCKY GRADES
DELIGHTFUL SCENERY
MILEAGE READS
SPRINGERVILLE & RICE
TO FT. APACHE
TO SNOWFLAKE & HOLBROOK
COOLEYS' RANCH
43.1 84.1
39.1 88.1
35. 92.2
31.7 95.5
CREEK
ROCKS
CREEK
ROCKS
CREEK
HAY FIELD
28. 99.2
CREEK
PINE FORESTS
H.C.
SUMMIT ELEVATION 9400 FT. H.C.
22. 105.2
H.C. ROCKS
19.4 107.8
H.C.
WATER
H.C.
OPEN PARK
17. 110.2
H.C.
ROCKS
H.C.
MILEAGE
WEST IN
EAST IN
N
13.4 113.8
ROUGH
12.5 114.7
10.2 117.
CINDER BED
6.1 121.1
R
4.7 122.5
3.7 121.5
FENCES
4.1 124.4
1. 126.2
EAGER
P.O.
2.4 126.1
1.9 126.6
SPRINGERVILLE
P.O. 000 127.2
TO MAGDALENA
G. BECKER'S STORE
LOOKING EAST
FRED COLTER RANCH

Left to right: Mrs. DeLamater with dog Teddy, Madeline Klinge, two Apaches, Dr. William DeLamater. The Copelands' Mitchell is in the background.

make our lunch on snaps are just 1½ miles from the right trail, very easy to get lost in this big pine forest its Uncle Sam's big perserve its miles and miles in length and breadth. About 4 P.M. come to a nice brook, here we decide to stay for the night. Mrs. D. & I wash out a few fearfully durty pieces. Fish hard for the pretty speckled trout but don't land any, we have a big camp fire and a nice time. cool so Guy and the Boys don their heavy underware, Guy has a bad tear in his pants so I mend it by the camp fire after he goes to bed.

June 6. Got up this morning to find it just 30 deg. ice frozen about ½ inch thick in a bucket frost on the ground [some fresh deer tracks near our camp] this is the White Mts. we don't feel very gay for the first thing is a steep hill, we ford the creek then unload our heaviest belongings. The Dr. gets to the top first, every body pushes all they can. Then we are pushed up reload and at 8 A.M. we go on, its up grade and so many boulders we don't make any headway but its still through that grand pine forest [Air is so thin neither people nor engines can work their full capacity.] we come to a large forest fire under controle but in one place a tree has fallen across the trail so we must make a new one. Well here is another very steep grade full of boulders get the Dr. up by the same old pushy method but tie a rope to a tree at the top then put it round our hub and all pull on the rope, are all tired out doing such stunts. We could now do very nicely if it wasn't for dodging "nigger heads" every 2 feet, we are almost to the divide when Mr. D. has a puncture its 12 noon we have been since 8 A.M. going 8 mile are not bothered with any one passing or meeting us. We would not advise a mongrel puppy to go overland from here in the east edge of Ariz. to the Pacific Ocean. we ate our lunch on the divide 9400 feet above sea level the highest point on the O to O highway here was where Mr. D.'s camped last Dec. for 7 day because they had a broken axle and the Dr. had to walk to Springerville, a distance of 25 miles here a blacksmith welded it for them they said it was 24 below zero and snow all over, we see snow now just off the trail a short ways. The road is just awful with large boulders. Now its a wet spot you get in then keep going, not out, but down The Dr. got through, Guy liked [ed. lacked] a little but we give him a big push, a few miles more then we strike a cinder road it sure looks good, it goes right apast an extinct volcano where they are getting the cinder for the road, its 4 P.M. only 6 miles to Springerville but below the hill the folks have some acquaintances, Mr. Hoffmans, they go down to call, soon the men are back have decided to camp down by their irrigating canal to night. Guy killed five bunnies in about half hour, the other folks went fishing. Mr. D.'s took supper with their friends; I fried 3 rabbits for our lunch to-morrow. we have been from 10 A.M. Monday June 2 to 4 P.M. Friday June 6 going 140 miles.

June 7. We got started about 7 A.M. At Springerville, Ariz. a little villiage 90 miles from a railroad we laid in some supplies [gasoline is 50 cts per gallon here] and about 8.30 A.M. started onward about 14 miles out we cross over into New Mexico, we

Springerville

Is the gateway of the Ocean-to-Ocean Highway from the East into Arizona, and junction of roads West to Roosevelt Dam and to the Petrified Forest and Grand Canyon.

G. BECKER'S MERCANTILE ESTABLISHMENT

The Traveling Public is cordially invited to come to G. Becker who will take pleasure in furnishing them all information regarding roads, Etc.

IN THE WHITE MOUNTAINS

Springerville is situated in a fine Stock Raising and Farming Country. Has excellent Trout Fishing and Hunting. Climate unsurpassed. The land of extinct volcanoes.

Guy Copeland and sons and the loaded Mitchell with an Arizona saguaro

are crossing the Datil Mts which are just one bench then another just higher The roads are not fine drives by any means only in comparison to what we have went over about 2 P.M. we have a blowout, the folk are way ahead but come back to get us about four P.M. the men stop [in some sage-brush] to shoot rabbits for a few minutes; get lost and are gone for over an hour After starting on we come to a sand wash here it was all hands pushey again and the clouds are getting thick too we go on about 6 miles where we must stop for the night as its raining a good shower and the wind is real strong, too, traveled about 60 miles today.

Apache passersby

III

Springerville, Arizona, to Raton, New Mexico

June 8-19

12 days, 463 miles, averaging less than 38.5 miles per day

Across New Mexico the travelers encountered a somewhat different set of obstacles and dangers, but their sense of peril in unfamiliar country remained the same. The environment caused them endless difficulties. If it was not sinking sand and steep grades, it was mud, washouts, and flooded arroyas. There were also mosquitoes. Even the signposts failed to reassure them, because they were told that Mexican bandits often turned them around in order to trap tourists. They found more towns in New Mexico than in Arizona, but they were Mexican towns, with unfamiliar customs and architecture, neither of which Estella Copeland found pleasing.

The Copelands probably began to feel somewhat encumbered by their companions during this stage of the trip. The DeLamater automobile suffered a tedious succession of calamities: within this twelve-day period this vehicle (of unknown manufacture) needed repairs to its frame, engine, brakes, "oiler," tires, and gears, causing altogether several days delay. The Copeland machine had only one blowout and a minor injury to its frame during this period. In addition to the DeLamaters' automobile trouble, Dr. DeLamater was almost continuously unwell, suffering from a back injury and a bout of malaria.

June 8. Sunday Morn. We don't look much like a Sunday crowd but all are well, but the Dr.'s back about 8 A.M. we started the first thing is a sand hill to go around here it took more pushey, have more sand than any thing else but are keeping out of the ruts; up grade most all the way, we got on the N.M. State Highway but that looks just like a very common road to us, eat our lunch in the National Forest there on a tree was the Ocean to Ocean Highway sign this road comes nearer looking like such a highway than any we have seen for a week. 1.30 P.M. we stop on account of a storm didn't rain much where we were, [Pass a well with good correl around it here you pay 5 cts. per head to water your stock. Didn't charge us any thing for drinking water, the lady was nice looking and seemed quiet intelligent;] camped in some pines about 13 miles from Magdalena.

June 9. Got in to Magdalena, early even if we did have a blow out just after we started, we find plenty of mud, about four miles from here is Kelly's Mines but they are not running now. This is the first railroad we have seen since just 20 miles out of Globe, Ariz. [just a week ago to day;] 24 miles to Socorro; roads are fine even if we do have the Magdalena Mountain Pass Eat our lunch in front of the Lady Magdalena Mt, one way you look at it its a lady's face, some boys climbed to the top and chisled a large M there. At Socorro I had to have my shoes half soled or go barefooted, the Men cleaned the Auto machienery. we got started about 3 P.M. are having plenty of sand would be having a time if it hadn't rained about 10 miles out we come to San Antonio cross the Rio Grande River on the railroad bridge, the sand is very bad and lots of it but being so damp we don't have to push very often; clouds are getting thick camp for the night hurry our supper on account of the rain and it surely did rain just after dark thought sure the tent would blow over but we didn't even get wet.

June 10. Reached Carthage early this A.M. have coal mines here; people most all Mexicans; [went into a store, (first, you went into a walled-up court)] Albuquerque is 97 miles away, right across the plains, most every stranger looses his road crossing this, very few signs then you can not tell whether these are right or not for the Mexicans change signs when-ever they like just to confuse the Americans, we got off our road once. [Miles and Miles out we came to a spring, where a shepherd was watering his sheep—hundreds and hundreds of them. This afternoon while fixing a tire a large machine came up, Mr. Story, millionaire piano man,[1] and his chaffaur, they are dressed like ourselves— very, very common. This trail offtimes takes us through dry creek beds for quiet a distance, up hill and down, across deep washes, or arroyas.] camped just 30 miles from Albuquerque could hardly get supper for the wind and showers had fine water from a spring.

June 11. This morn we find we have some neighbors an auto with two men going to Ariz. fishing. We had gone but short ways when came on to a flock of ducks. About 6 miles from Albuquerque come to an arroya with water just rushing Guy took off shoes and socks waded in to see if we could get across, put on our chains it was an awful pull but we got through. In Albuquerque, Mr. D. had their [broken] Auto [frame] mended, we got away about 3 P.M. This may be a nice city but what we saw was more Mexican than American. Mr. D. had a blowout right on one of their dreadful narrow streets, they throw all their tin cans bottles and such like right in the street. Camped about 15 miles out, the misquetoes almost carried us off we were in the Rio Grande River valley and it is irrigated.

June 12. To Santa Fe is 64 miles up grade all the way have sand and wash outs, too, have alkali water. Therefore have a time with hot engines. Don't do much road work out here but we did come to a gang of convicts at work on the road [were

---

[1] Possibly Edward Hampton Story, president of the Story and Clark Piano Company in Chicago. He died in 1939 at age seventy-three. *New York Times,* September 4, 1939.

doing it well one place they had cut the roadway through a hill.] At 10 A.M. came to Domingo a railroad station its an [Pueblo] Indian trading station. Here we got to take an Indian picture Them in Mr. D.'s Auto they wanted 2 bits we gave them a dime; they are friendly Indians. The arroya here is up and rushing but we decide to try it. Indians came down you should have seen them sling moccasins, but we didn't need any help. Went on a few miles farther forded the Santa Fe Creek then climbed the La Bajada Hill a lava hill which was some thing like this[2] twice we had to back to make the turns [nothing to keep you from backing off, then down, down, down on a pile of rock; at the top is a table-land of many, many acres of grazing land. Its mostly up grade, our engines heat but we, at last reach Santa Fe.] Just after we passed the Capotal Building Mr. D. had a blow out that had to be mended right there; this is a queer looking city, very narrow streets, and dirty, late afternoon we get out of the city, climbing hills as we go, camp among the pines [on the Glorieta Mountains] about 7 miles out.

June 13. Fri. and the 13th first thing we did was to think we were on the wrong road, come back and start on another with a very high rough hill to climb Mr. D. going first their break refused to work, tell you there came near being an accident, [they were going at the rate of something like 25 miles per hour when they got to the foot] when we all got to the foot of the hill we decided to take the other road which proved to be the right one [there is the gate to open that our guide book says we will find, so we know we are on the right road.] About 2 P.M. Mr. D. has trouble with their oiler we are delayed about 2 hours go just a few miles more when they have a blow out its not far from Starvation Peak so called because in early days the Indians chased some Mexicans upon it there was only one way to get up it the Indians guarded that and as the Mexican were without food or water they soon

---

[2] Here Estella Copeland draws a twisty, curvy line.

"We come to a swift running arroya at the edge of a genuine Mexican village." June 13, 1913

starved . . . We don't go far till we find a part of the road way washed out all got out and we got around O.K. [but a broken auto told that someone failed to get by, farther on came to where the trail was so badly washed try to straddle it but slip down in, the fly-wheel struck, had to shovel our way out and for quiet a distance.] Next we come to a swift running arroya at the edge of a genuine Mexican village we got through. Just think right here in the U.S. a whole village that didn't know enough English to hardly tell you where to find a drink of water, [here a small granite monument marking the old Santa Fe Trail] while we were there the goat herder brought in the goats but we didn't wait to see them milked. we camped about 8 miles from Las Vegas.

June 14. [Were awaken before day-break by a Mexican wood-hauler passing whistling "Cassey Jones";] get to town about 8.30 came through mud and washes Las Vegas seemed to us to be larger than Albuquerque. [Get out few miles when Mr. D.'s have engine trouble which delays us for long while, sun beats down so hot, finally on the go now is mud, then to the river, can't get across man tell us go through a gate, along the bank, cross an alfalfa field, autos almost stand on end going down a bank, through a low place, up bank into the village of Watrous] Roads are muddy at 2 P.M. we get to Watrous just 20 miles from Las Vegas, here the river is so high can not get across, decide to camp here till the water runs down being in a mountainous country it does so very quickly. The elevation here is between 6000 and 7000 feet above sealevel. Guy found a nice pen-knife, I claim it. [Learn that June is N.M. rainy season and that a week ago had quiet a flood. Mr. Story's auto is on a freight car, he is shipping 60 miles to Springer. We camp in villiage park near one river].

June 15. Still in camp, across the street from us is Dr. Goble a former Hoosier, we get acquainted he brought us over quiet a bunch of Indianapolis News.

June 16. At noon they pulled us across the Moore River [each Auto paid $2] only went 6½ miles when big rain caught us; at about 1½ miles farther Mr. D. insisted we leave them and get out of the wet they hadn't chain, we had. [we go only a few miles till there has been no rain; road fairly good but this is a grazing country so we have some gates to open] Camped 10 miles this side North of Wagon mound.

June 17. Went only 5½ miles when come to the river and couldn't get across are advised to go back about 2½ miles take another road for Colmar there could find a team to pull us over. [This is a mountain stream not very wide but a rain in the mountains often causes it to raise 15 feet in half an hour] Mr. D. run about ½ mile on the railroad but we would not take that risk at 12.30 started across hitched behind a wagon that way ment slick high bank on the up side finelly [they take the wagon away &] hitched 4 horses on [to the Auto] they didn't pull together then went and got block and tackle got out that way at 3.30 P.M. [cost $1.50] Run till about dark, so could ford the river near the town of French, forded it O.K. [out bounced our medicine satchel also sack of ginger cakes, damage a broken alcohol bottle.] Then camped, Then we found we needed to dry things that were in our trunk on the back of

LOG OF PUBLIC ROAD FROM SPRINGERVILLE, ARIZ. TO ALBUQUERQUE, N. M.

(This log made and furn'shed by *Butler Auto Co., Albuquerque, N. M.*)

SPRINGERVILLE, ARIZ.

Depart 8:30 A. M.

0.0 Becker Mercantile Co. Store.
1.1 Forks; bear left.
1.9 Forks; bear left across creek, thence up a grade.
4.1 Forks; bear left.
6.6 Top hill.
7.7 Forks; bear left.
7.9 Forks; bear right.
10.3 Forks; bear left.
10.4 Forks; both roads same.
11.7 Both roads come in together.
12.0 Forks; bear left.
14.2 Cross small dry creek.
15.2 Forks; bear right; left road leads to Salt Lakes.
15.4 Cross road.
22.3 Cross road.
26.1 Pinon hill.
26.3 Forks; bear right down hill.
31.6 Cross road.
34.3 Blanis Lake on left.
34.8 Forks; bear left.
43.2 Pass two dry lakes.
45.5 Along small timber.
47.6 Out of canon.
48.1 Forks; bear left.

This guide required close attention to the speedometer to check how far the motorist had come since the previous landmark.

the Auto. [We are all almost worn out with what we have went through to day.]

June 18. Got nice early start only run till about 8 A.M. find a washout Mr. D. chew their gears some & Miss Madeline got stuck in quick sand had to be shoveled out got it repaired so could run went about a mile there another washout and a car badly stuck in the mud almost to the axle, try to help them, have to jack up the back wheels put pieces under and all pull on our rope put round his back hub after long and hard work he went out of the mud hole but there is almost straight up bank, hadn't got up that yet when sight a span of mules its noon the man hired them to help him up the grade he had a 6 cylinder 60 h.p. Locomobile; he hired the man with the team to stay and help us repair the bridge we got through, ate lunch then started about 2 P.M. About 10 miles from Raton Mr. D.'s gears take another chew. They repair them so we could run 3 miles more [to Red River] we will camp here till they get new gears Just had time to get our tents up when are in a heavy rain, Two

The Mitchell often had to be towed across flooded arroyas and streams.

[Colorado] young men enroute to Prescott, Ariz. camp by us, have a fine time [around our big, driftwood camp fire].

June 19. Could not get the gears out, so tighten all bolts and start for Raton, [camp on the commons of Raton N.M. near the brick factory;] unloaded our tenting outfit put up our tents then the men start for town, we find that the frame of our machine is broken. About 11.30 A.M. have very heavy rain Burl has a spell of indigestion. Our Auto comes back to camp at 5:30 P.M. all repaired. Have to send to Kansas City for gear for Mr. D.'s machine. Most beautiful sunset on the Rocky Mts. with clouds and two rainbows. Dr. very sick this afternoon; malarah.

IV

Raton, New Mexico, to Olustee, Oklahoma

June 20–July 2

12 days, 9 days traveling, averaging about 102+ miles per day

The Copelands waited with the DeLamaters in Raton for three days, until the new gears arrived from Kansas City. The day after the group finally set off again the DeLamater automobile developed more engine troubles, and at this point the Copelands left them and went on alone.

Once they were through the Rockies the family found good roads and made reasonably good time. The Copelands' tires were worn out and the weather was very warm, so they were delayed often by blowouts. They also broke a spring, a repair that proved difficult to make successfully since the same spring broke several more times before they were home.

Estella Copeland noted on June 21, while they were still camped in Raton waiting for gears, that they had pancakes for breakfast, a rare treat during this trip. Most mornings of course there had been something of a rush to finish a quick breakfast and return to the journey. William Copeland, the eleven-year-old who had been nauseated for five days early in the trip, reported in later years that he still disliked rolled oats for breakfast because he had eaten them so often on the overland trip. "The oats were cooked in a tin molasses bucket over the camp fire," his son William Copeland, Jr., reported from

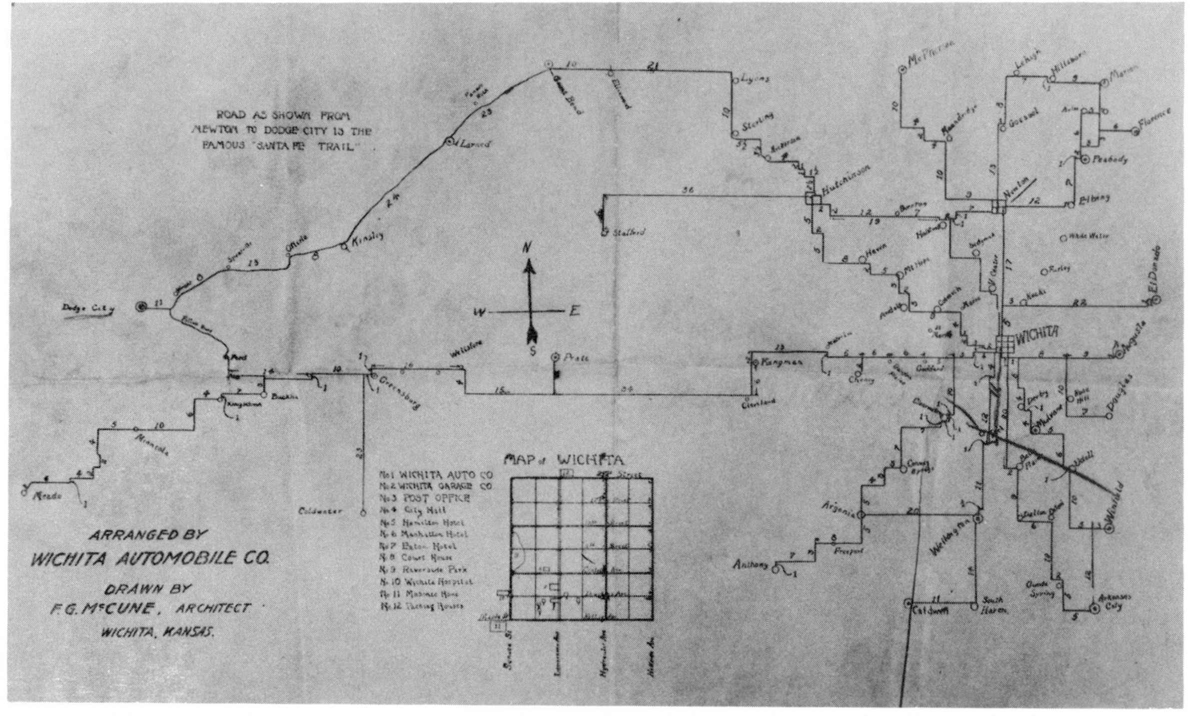

This schematic map shows the route the Copelands followed from Dodge City to Wichita.

family tradition, "with a resulting scorch on the bottom of the thin metal."

June 20. Roads are drying and they say they are working on the washouts ahead of us. This is a railroad shop town of about 6,000 and several coal mining camps not far away. About dark a young man rode up to camp had quiet a little visit, said he was from Vermont [had asthma] brought here last December on a stretcher by his wife, trained nurse, and doctor now feels fine working in a store. Had a very hard wind just after we went to bed wasn't a very hard rain.

June 21. Made pancakes for breakfast. [Have some callers to-day so learn something of our camping spot.] Are camped in sight of two large Mesas one 9 miles away the other 12 mi. the larger one is 9 mi. by 12 miles do not need to fence them on account of the rim rock that means that it is straight down for 150 ft. (something like this[1]) before it begins to slope, stock will drift with a storm, one time there was a sever storm from the North on this large mesa the cowboys tried every way to turn their stock but could not and they plunged over the rim rock 17,000 head lay piled up dead. Gears didn't come today.

June 22. Young Vermont man made us a call this A.M., his name is Benton Staples, brought his wife this P.M. Mr. D.'s gears came.

June 23. Left at 6 A.M. first thing is climb the Rockies called the Raton Pass; good road banasters at steep places, found the richest colored wild flowers ever saw There were all colors represented, the locust we found was sort of a shrub with lavander colored blossom which did not have that fainty-sick odor like Hoosier locust. this is our 7th and last mountain range, have a fine view of the snowy peaks crossed the Colo.

[1] Here Estella Copeland draws a rough diagramatic sketch of the rim rock and slope.

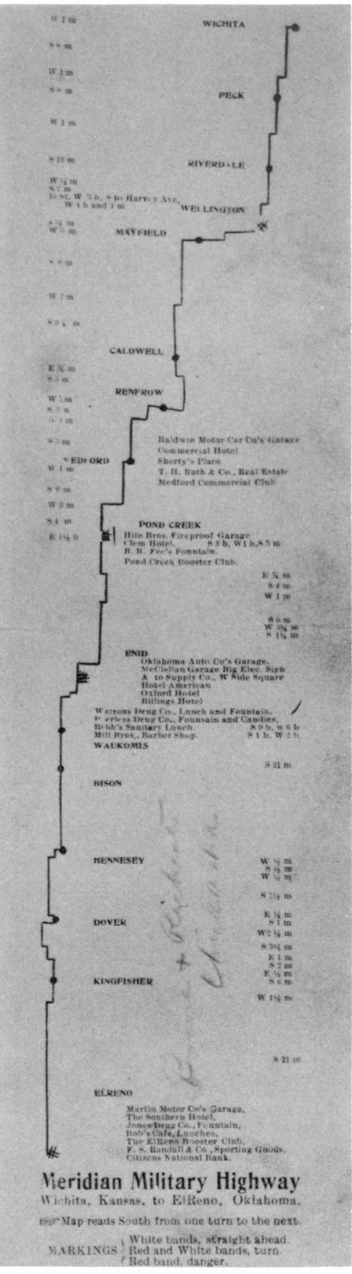

Wichita, Kansas, to
El Reno, Oklahoma

and New Mexico State line at an elevation of 8976 feet got into Trinidad, Colo. about 9.30 A.M. got some repairs then got out on good roads. Mr. D.'s have much engine trouble, we have a blowout or two. don't make much time.

June 24. Still going across praire very good road, getting warmer, have some blowouts reach La Junta at noon, Mr. D.'s work on their engine, start out [at 3 P.M. only go a few blocks] it doesn't do any better, so we leave them, [they say for us to go on they will soon overtake us, but they had a bad master-coil so never caught up with us.] this is a fine irrigated country, camped at a school-house.

June 25. Roads are fine; reached Syracuse Kan. at noon, got to Garden City and camped in edge of town by the largest Individual Mule Market in the world.

June 26. Got an early start reached Great Bend about 6 P.M. got gasoline had made about 140 miles were almost out of town when broke a spring at street crossing, found a blacksmith to weld it, got out to the edge of town it broke again run back to garage, Guy and Boys slept on the cots, I in the machine, very warm.

June 27. Got our spring welded, left at 9 A.M. fine roads, got off our road at Ellinwood there we followed the old Santa Fe Trail (which is marked with red, white & blue) were out of McPherson about 2½ miles when found out we should have taken the New Santa Fe Trail (which is marked by white bands [on telephone poles]) to Newton went back to McPherson then down to Newton [just 400 miles from Olustee very warm but we have to pump up tires every few miles.] this is a beautiful town, finest dwellings, did not see any commons and were looking for some to camp on, found a place about 5 miles out, at a cross-roads.

June 28. [Today, think must have been chigers we heard about our cots, last night, instead of bunnies] Wichita is only 25 miles from Newton so we soon reach it; is very warm, wheat is being thrashed, have much trouble with patches melting off

Guy's brother Charles and their mother Nancy
Copeland

our inner tubes, are directed wrong and get to Breman, then we start out going South and West on the most traveled roads till we find out we are only 18 miles from Medford have went about 30 miles out of our way stop at Garage for instructions [Get instructions from one garage to the next town is the way we are guided through this state] and a tire went flat so run inside put in another tube and it leaked, bought a small gasoline vulcanizer, repaired the tube by that time its raining and when thats over its dark so we spent the night in the garage (look too much like gypsies to go to a hotel) Have quite a visit with a Civil War vetern who is blind on account of the war lost one eye then and other was so effected he has been blind for 20 odd years, he was with Sherman on his march to the sea, he told of the Battle of Peach Tree Creek, one regiment (the largest there, in number) charged three times, last time came back in disorder then the General ordered this man's regiment the 82nd Ohio and an Indiana regiment to unite and make the charge which they did and won the battle but the cost to life was heavy.

June 29. Left about 8.30 A.M. had a flat tire at about 3

The Charles Copelands and the Louds in front of their store in Olustee

miles, roads are fairly good some rolling [vulcanized tubes while eating our dinner; soil is red as blood] camped about 3½ miles from El Reno.

June 30. Started 6.30 roads rather sandy a young fellow and span of mules just stays at the Canadian River to pull folks through the sandy bottom charged a dollar; have very rolling ground got to Lawton at dusk clouds are low and very dark, just got into Thompson Garage when had a very, very hard rain spread out cots for the night.

July 1. Left Garage about 10 A.M. only run to the edge of town when pull into an unused side street to wait for the mud to dry. left about 1 O'clock, bad running for about 12 miles so muddy. Had to be pulled across a ford near Cashe; [pay $.50 Just out of Snyder crossed 8 bridges in going 1 mile.] camped about 4 miles west of Snyder.

July 2. Started 6.15 A.M. for Olustee 36 miles away; arrived 9.30 A.M. first thing was to get some dirt off. . . .

V

Olustee, Oklahoma, to Greenwood, Indiana

July 14-24

11 days, 1,191.3 miles, averaging 108+ miles per day

With what relief Nancy Wells Copeland and the Charles Copelands greeted Guy and his family has not been recorded. The journey from Watsonville to Olustee had taken seven weeks, eight days of which were taken up with layovers in Glendale, Brawley, and Raton.

The Copelands rested for twelve days at Olustee, no doubt regaling their relatives with lively accounts of western adventures and admiring Charles Copeland's home and business.

They continued on their journey in mid-July and, unsurprisingly, traveled in extremely hot, dry weather through most of Oklahoma and Kansas. The heat played havoc with their worn-out, patched tires and innertubes, so they replaced the tires in Wichita. Their journey was basically a smooth one: there were bridges or ferries available for crossing rivers and streams and friendly residents to offer them assistance along the way. The anxious note disappears from Estella's entries as she re-enters familiar territory.

The Mitchell developed a few kinks running greater distances at higher speeds on substantially better roads than it was used to. The engine balked completely near Marshall, Missouri, and required a thorough cleaning by a mechanic before it could continue.

July 14. Left Olustee 10 A.M. [these hot winds are terrible, at Snyder get ice in our desert water-bag.] road hot and dry till east of Indiahoma camped about 15 miles North of Lawton traveled about 90 mi.

July 15. Started 8 A.M. cannot travel very fast too much tire trouble it seems to be getting hotter and dryer camped just north of El Reno [in school yard among billions of mosquitos, to sing us a lullaby.] went about 90 miles.

July 16. Started 6.45 A.M. about 11 A.M. reached Hennesey, Oklahoma here in the little town park is a grand, large, brown, stone monument erected in honor of the only Oklahoma soldier killed in the Spanish-American War this was his home town. camped 14 miles north east of Medford traveled about 110.

July 17. Started 6.45 A.M. [Go only a few miles when cross the Oklahoma-Kansas State Line near Caldwell, Kansas] very hot winds corn badly burned, old tires give much trouble hope they last till we get to Wichita; which they did, there we bought new ones [one fine thing—can carry ice for almost 24 hours in our desert water-bag] camped 6 miles from Newton.

July 18. Started 6.15 had splendid luck found the roads good, mostly rolling about 6 O'clock when we were at Williamsburg saw a very dark cloud gathering in the North West we out run it to Ottawa 17 miles the rain was comming down real hard when we reached the first garage, the man was very accomidating told us to make our selves at home we spread our cots and did so, he took me over to call on his wife we had a nice visit and she gave me a big loaf of home-made bread. We run 150 miles.

July 19. Started 7.15 [cross a swinging bridge, which wiggles like a snake] had some trouble with our old inner tubes but got to Kansas City about 3.15 P.M. must have been more than 5 P.M. when we got out of City, on good macadamized road but Indipendence Mo. seems to be just a Suburb of Kansas City. got our first view of the Missouri River at Wellington,

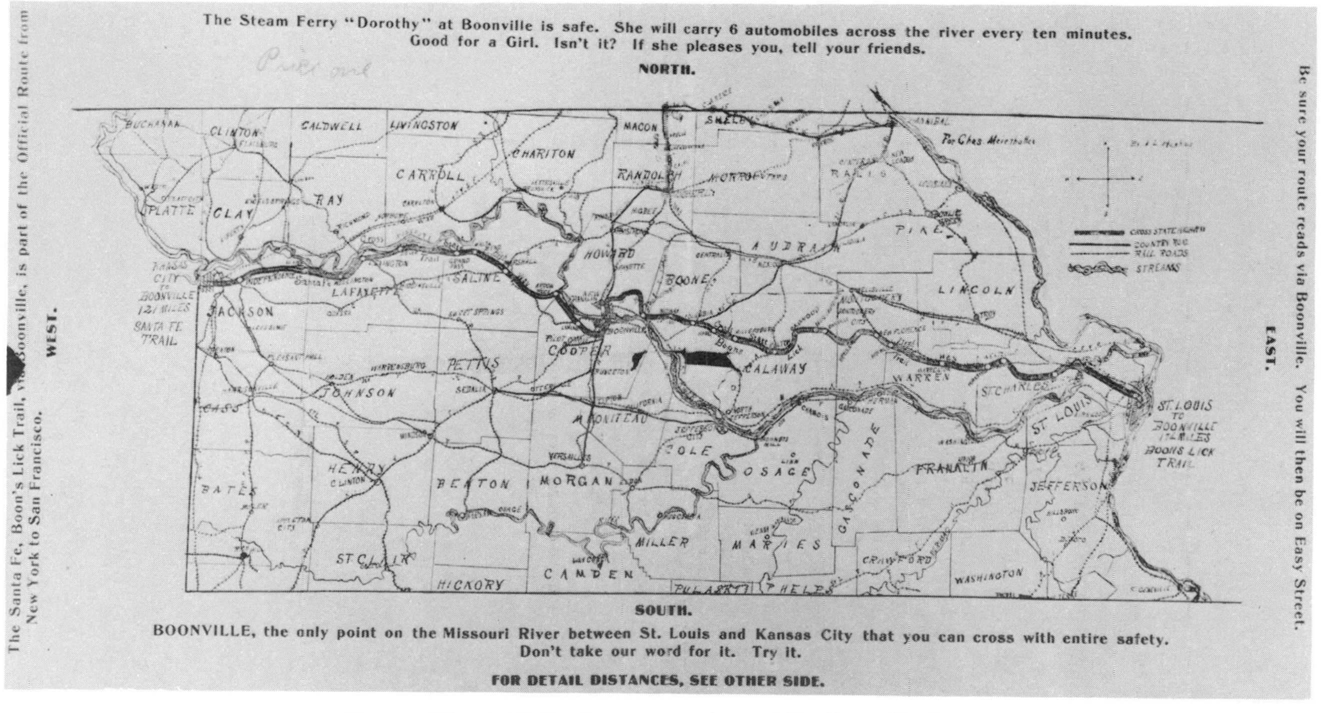

Kansas City to St. Louis, map courtesy of the Boonville ferry

NATIONAL OLD TRAIL ROAD OCEAN TO OCEAN HIGHWAY

A Guide and Directory for Automobile Tourists for 1913

On the Ocean to Ocean Highway Trail Between St. Louis, Missouri, and Indianapolis, Indiana.

This Guide is Given Away Free of Charge at any Garage that has their Advertisement in this Book.

This Guide has been gotten out especially to accommodate the tourist people, and we would advise the tourist people to call on these firms who have their ad in this Guide, and we assure you that your patronage will be highly appreciated by all of them.

If you are touring east of Indianapolis, Ind., to Columbus, Ohio, via the Ocean to Ocean Highway Trail, you exchange this Guide for a new one for that part of the trail at the Claypool Garage, 27-33 N. Capitol Ave., in Indianapolis, Ind.

If you are touring west of St. Louis, Mo., to Kansas City, Kansas, on the Ocean to Ocean Highway Trail, you exchange this Guide for a new one for that part of the trail at the Cabany Motor Co., Salesroom & Garage 526-34 De Baliviere Ave., in St. Louis, Mo.

These Guides Are Free To All Automobile Tourists.

This Guide and Directory is Gotten Out by

CHAS. EVANS & CO.,

EFFINGHAM, - - - ILLINOIS

run along in sight of or by it to Lexington Mo. getting late so camp at a school-house about 3 miles out of town, run about 116 miles.

July 20. Started about 7 A.M. everything went well till about 9 A.M. when engine stopped and would not go with all Kinds of coaxing, so a Mr. Walker came along in his machine and Guy went home with him and telephoned to Keys & Blosser Garage at Marshall Mo. ten miles away to come pull us in, [which they did at noon,] got in they found a machinest he cleaned the breaker box by soaking it in gasoline then adjusted its points put it all together and it went off all right [18 miles we come to the little old time village of Arrow Rock here was an old fashion Inst.] its 38 miles to Boonville where we take the ferry across the Missouri River but it doesn't make a trip after 6 P.M. so we were 15 minutes too late went up on a hill at edge of town and camped. Boonville is a river town of about 6,000 population.

July 21. First ferry leaves at 7 A.M. we are on hands, the trip across was nice just cost $1.00 we found the road hilly, culberts in bad shape. had a flat tire about 2 miles out of Trusdale right in front of a lovely home got to talking with the man his name was D.C. Hageman he was raised near Vevy, Ind. and is related to the Clarkes & Wintrows in Johnson Co. Ind. we camped at a school house about a mile from his home and just about 55 miles from St. Louis.

July 22. Started about 6.30 A.M. when we got to St. Charles here we cross the Missouri river again but on a toll bridge this time, cost 45 cts. reached the outskirts of St. Louis about 10.30 A.M. at 3.15 were out to the edge of Troy about 21 miles out when broke our same old spring were 4 miles from interurban line so put a block of wood under and run back but its too late to get into the city before the stores close so we get to camp in a farmer's orchard very fine people.

July 23. Guy left on the 5.30 A.M. car for St. Louis got back put the new leaf of the spring on and we left at 11 A.M. [This is

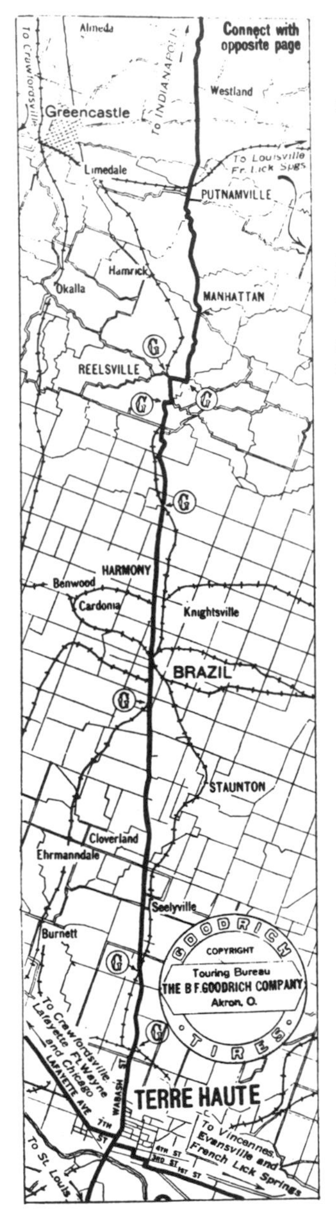

ROUTE 119.

TERRE HAUTE TO INDIANAPOLIS.

Gravel and Macadam.

Miles

0.0 TERRE HAUTE. East on Wabash St. Cross R. R.

2.6 Under R. R. Straight on.

5.5 Ⓖ Cross R. R.

7.4 Ⓖ Cross R. R. Cross R. R thru Seelyville.

14.4 Ⓖ Cross R. R. Again at

15.1 BRAZIL. (R). Straight thru

18.3 HARMONY. Thru covered bridge.

20.2 Turn right, across R. R. bridge.

22.7 Ⓖ Cross R. R. Again Ⓖ, 23.5.

24.2 REELSVILLE. Ⓖ Turn right.

24.5 Ⓖ Turn left at crossroads.

26.6 MANHATTAN. (Ⓖ Road on left leads to GREENCASTLE.) Straight on for Indianapolis.

30.3 PUTNAMVILLE. Cross R. R. bridge.

36.3 MT. MERIDIAN. Straight on, passing Goodrich Marker on left.

43.4 STILESVILLE. Straight thru

51.6 BELLVILLE. Cross trolley and concrete bridge, thru

56.4 PLAINFIELD. (R). Straight on.

60.3 Ⓖ Cross R. R. Thru HOBBS and

61.3 BRIDGEPORT. Straight on. Under R. R. Follow trolley on Washington St., crossing R. Rs. Turn left on Capitol Ave.

70.4 INDIANAPOLIS. Goodrich Building, Capitol Ave. and Michigan St. See City Map for connection to SPEEDWAY

CALL AT

Goodrich Building

INDIANAPOLIS

(H)—Hotel.
(R)—Repair and Gasoline Stop.
Ⓖ—Goodrich Road Marker.

The *Goodrich Route Book* offered a more detailed guide than most the Copelands had used. [p. 127]

The Copeland homestead on their return

the Old National Road some of the old "corduroy" is visible yet, not much road work being done.] Stopped at a farm house, about two miles east of Effingham, Ill., to get water it being about dark and time to camp we were invited to camp in their barn-lot which we did; in the night we were awaken by the rain spattering in our faces [(we have not put up the tent for many nights)] so we hustled our cots in the barn and the dog got after us so we went to the auto and slept with the children.

July 24. Started out at 5:30 A.M. roads are not very good till come to the Indiana State line then its gravel or macadam greater part macadam; about noon time are at Brazil, Ind. Auto refuses to go right on Main St. Guy cleaned the breaker-box with gasoline and we were O.K. again. got into Indianapolis about 5 P.M. distance of 135 miles from starting place this A.M. after making a few calls on old friends we reach Milton's about dark, surprised them away from the supper table.

Thus the long journey is done.

greater part macadam; about noon time
are at Brazil Ind. auto refuses to go
right on Main St. Guy cleaned the breaker
box with gasoline and we were O.K. again.
got into Indianapolis about 5. P.M. distance
of 135 miles from starting place this A.M.
after making a few calls on old friends
we reach Miltons about dark, surprised
them away from the supper table.

Thus the long journey is done.

~~235~~ 332 gal, gasoline 18 to 45 per gal = 78.22.
12½ " lubricating ~~40~~ 50 1.10 per gal. $9.85
4000 miles
~~8~~

assistance .50
2.00
1.50
.50
1.00
5.50

Crossing river 1.00
45
45
7.40

Last page of diary

332 gal. gasoline	18 to 45[¢] per gal. =	[$]78.22
12½ " lubricating	50 [to] 1.10 per gal. =	$ 9.85

4000 miles[1]

assistance

	.50
	2.00
	1.50
	.50
	1.00
	[$]5.50

Crossing rivers

	1.00
	.45
	.45
	[$]1.90

[1] This figure may have included some traveling in California before the trip home. The distance traveled, without including wrong turns, was closer to 3,780 miles.

Postscript

Upon returning to Indiana Guy Copeland once again took up farming on the family homestead. He purchased cattle and a wagon, and not long after his return began to construct a drying barn for his anticipated new crop—tobacco. However, the tobacco venture failed, and the following year he converted the barn into housing for the livestock. Guy continued to show an interest in scientific experiments—for example, building a carbide gas plant for lighting their home.

Guy and Estella's children, William H. and Burl D., also farmed as an occupation. William married Clarice Dressler on August 3, 1930, and they had two children, Eva Louise and William, Jr., the owners of the materials used for this book. Burl was married to Mary Ann McClain on August 1, 1929, and their children were Donald Burl, Charles Richard, George Edgar, John Mahlon, and Larry Bruce. William Copeland, Jr., and his cousins George and John have continued to farm the Copeland homestead to the present day.

The Copelands did not put their family camping days altogether behind them upon their return. In the early 1920s, they unpacked the old tent and set off with their now grown-up sons for a trip to Grand Haven, Michigan. The older son

The Copelands camping in Michigan in the 1920s

Guy and Estella, 1933

William Copeland posed for an Arizona newspaper on his trip west in 1950.

in turn drove his family to Tucson, Arizona, in the winter of 1950. Then both the sons and their families camped out to California, retracing the earlier journey, and even found part of an old log road—the corduroy road—in California.

By the 1950s a family automobile tour of the west was one of the most popular American vacations, offering magnificent scenery, striking examples of cultural diversity, and well-equipped campgrounds at frequent intervals. Western state and federal highways were among the nation's proudest accomplishments, and the rigors faced by pioneer automobile tourists like the Copelands had long been replaced by relative ease and comfort. Many adventurers still sought rugged natural settings in which to test their skills and endurance, but for most families the aim was like that of the Copelands in 1913—to see some beautiful and exotic countryside while traveling relatively inexpensively. The accommodations these later family tourists found were a result of the pioneering journeys of people like the Copelands who demonstrated a need for them.

John Giles

Donald Copeland (l.) and William H. Copeland, Jr., sons of Burl and William Copeland, respectively, posed with an unrestored 1910 Mitchell owned by Robert DeRees of Indianapolis in April, 1980.